Think Outside the Bottle:
The Product Entrepreneur's
Playbook

by Duane Thompson with Cheryl Ross

© Copyright 2016 Duane Thompson

ISBN 978-0-99701-630-7

Published by

SabRoss Publishers

THINK OUTSIDE THE BOTTLE

The Product Entrepreneur's Playbook

DUANE THOMPSON

with Cheryl Ross

TABLE OF CONTENTS

PREFACE

YEARS AGO, WHEN I was first trying to make my way as a product entrepreneur, a rep at the local Small Business Development Center looked at me like I had six arms when I revealed I was selling a product—one that I was growing, manufacturing, and distributing locally—not a service. She was surprised to learn I was selling a special–recipe blend I'd perfected in my own kitchen—and she wasn't the only one. Others, including friends, wanted to know why I was investing so much time trying to launch a salsa when I already had a very well–paying job. Given the dramatic decrease in product manufacturing in the United States over the last several decades and our culture's emphasis on working for others, it's no wonder people were perplexed.

To answer their question, I told them I make and sell salsa for a personal reason and because I strongly believe the US needs more product entrepreneurs who create and sell their own goods. I want to help this country reinvigorate product manufacturing. It's about building a stronger US dollar and making the US sustainable. As the old saying goes, "It starts with me."

So I've written *Think Outside the Bottle: The Product Entrepreneur's Playbook* to help Americans who have created a product, dream to create a product, or have a product in the works. I want to see more of us introduce new products into the marketplace—products created, produced, manufactured, and sold in the States. *Think Outside the Bottle* can help you find success while also helping our country.

A little history: In the course of running my own product business, I've tried to understand the scope of US product manufacturing by researching its decline over past decades, and as result, its impact on the US economy. The info I gleaned jarred me. I cannot get some of the stats out of my mind.

Bureau of Labor Statistics show just how damaging product manufacturing losses have been to the US. Between 1970 and 2009, US goods–producing jobs shrank from 39 percent of the private–sector workforce to 17 percent. Meanwhile, we've had to borrow more to pay for things made elsewhere, and wouldn't you know it, middle–class workers have suffered the most. Service–sector jobs that replaced manufacturing jobs paid an average weekly wage of $610, compared with $810 in the goods–producing sector. Between 2000 and 2009 alone, median household incomes dropped 4 percent because of the disappearance of solid manufacturing jobs.

If you didn't see why a push to increase product manufacturing in the US was important before, I hope these startling stats help you now understand. To become a financially stronger country, the US needs to get back to creating *and* manufacturing more of its own goods.

But still, while you may want to *create* a product, and you may agree with me that this would boost US manufacturing and innovation, maybe you're not convinced that *manufacturing* your own product in America is a good business move *for you* (there is a difference between creating and manufacturing, which you'll learn about as you get deeper into this book). You may be thinking, *Why should I choose a US manufacturer when there could be less expensive options overseas?* First, depending on the type of product you're making, working with overseas manufacturers won't necessarily be less expensive. And that's just for starters.

Shipping products from overseas can be very expensive, and once a product reaches the States, it still has to be shipped around the country to customers, which means you're paying foreign *and* domestic shipping costs.

Another consideration is speed of delivery. Weather or unexpected travel accidents can delay overseas shipments, which means postponed sales; or your products could get damaged during long periods of travel.

Durable goods, like food products, are especially vulnerable.

Another demerit: It is harder to supervise overseas production—that's if you're able to supervise production at all. You'll either have to frequently visit the manufacturing site or send someone from your company (either for frequent visits or to live) to oversee every step of the process. Consider that there may be a language barrier between you and your manufacturer too. If you or your traveling employee don't know the manufacturer's language, you have to hope and trust that at least one of the manufacturer's staffers—for your sake, one who knows enough about your product to watch over the manufacturing process—speaks fluent English.

Some of the benefits of manufacturing in the States should now be obvious—communication issues between you and your manufacturer should be minimal, if any; by doing business domestically, and especially if your manufacturer is in the same area as your business, you can transport your products to your customers at the lowest price in the shortest time, which can mean higher sales and profits and fewer logistical headaches. And if you care about the impact of your business decisions on our country's economy as well as your business's bottom line, then this should make you smile: Manufacturing in the States can create more jobs here and a better environment for selling your product. More people with jobs is more people who have the resources to buy your goods.

The importance of being an American product entrepreneur can't be overstated. In this role, you have the potential to fortify our economy with jobs and paychecks. You can create an economic ripple that lifts all ships. Now that we've put this topic in its proper place, let's get down to brass tacks. Let's lift the economy by helping you become a successful product entrepreneur.

—*Duane Thompson*
President and CEO, Sabrosa Foods Inc.
Norfolk, VA
www.sabrosafoods.com

INTRODUCTION

CONGRATULATIONS ON PICKING up *Think Outside the Bottle: The Product Entrepreneur's Playbook*. If you're a product entrepreneur who means business, you're holding the key to success in your hands. One warning before we get started: If your product doesn't change lives, put this book down right now, because no amount of advice will help you succeed.

By changing lives, I don't necessarily mean saving people's lives or making them rich (but certainly, if you have a product that does these things, you've got something!). No, the product could change someone's life in some small way that is weighty and important to them. And even a product that solves a small problem could mean big business for you. I know this firsthand.

In *Think Outside the Bottle*, I'll share how I turned my salsa, Asorbas, into a profit maker in less than a decade. You may be wondering how a salsa changed anyone's life—even in a small way. Well, Asorbas has.

In *Think Outside the Bottle*, you'll learn what led me to create the salsa and the specific steps I took to make it profitable; I want you to pick up cues from my success story and apply them to your own product launch. You'll also encounter guides on how to develop your product, select a brand name and image, create a business plan, choose the right manufacturer, and publicize your product *for free*. You'll learn why you need a mentor; receive a refresher course on business lessons you picked up in other jobs that can help you succeed now; why it pays to launch your product in your own community and state; why you should only sell one product initially; why you must be self-aware in order to avoid traps that could lead to failure; and why thinking outside the bottle will *always* pay dividends to your business venture.

You'll want to have highlighters, Post–it Notes, and pens to mark up this book and rely on it over and over as you prepare to take your product to the marketplace. Not only should you mark up chapters, at the end of each one you'll also want to brainstorm and take notes in a feature called "Thinking Outside the Bottle."

Consider this book a business mentor in paper format (or electronic, if you're reading it on an e–device). Heck, even consider it a best friend, one that wants to encourage you to take your product to the next level. *Think Outside the Bottle* can help you create it, develop it, manufacture it, sell it, and find success.

Solving a Problem

So how has Asorbas changed lives? We need to answer this question and make a few other key points before we leap into the book. You'll soon see how what I'm about to tell you all comes back to you and your product.

So, Asorbas . . . Plenty of people love chips and salsa. Plenty of people also suffer from acid reflux and heartburn, and we know that if you want to avoid these conditions, avoid salsa (or take an anti–heartburn or acid reflux pill). At least that used to be the case . . . before Asorbas. Asorbas lets you enjoy your chips or omelette without necessarily having to reach for a pill. How? Swapping out tomatoes for red bell peppers as the main ingredient diminishes the salsa's acidity.

Want to have your bowl of chips without the heartburn? Look no further than Asorbas.

As Asorbas was rolled out everywhere from arts and crafts fairs to farmers' markets in the mid to late 2000s, its unique selling point (for many people, eating it without worrying about an attack of acid reflux or heartburn) and the fact that many consumers loved its taste gave it a leg up on its competition. By solving a problem *and* being delicious, Asorbas stood out among a large field of worthy opponents.

Something else gave it an edge: People were buying *me* before they bought my salsa. Put another way, *people have to buy you before they buy your product.* This goes hand in hand with producing a product that solves a problem. Let me explain:

To succeed in the marketplace, your product has to solve a problem *and* you have to connect with consumers. It's your personal story—the reason you launched your product—that allows you to commiserate and connect with people and make the sale. The problem your product solves should result from an experience that moved you, changed you, or from your very own need for what you're selling. Your story should allow you to address who you are and demonstrate why you created your product and what your product solves. If it doesn't do these things, you've got a problem.

You see, I made a winning product, and I also had a winning story—this was the win–win combo that gave Asorbas a decent shot at sales success. I didn't create Asorbas because I thought it would make me a millionaire. I created it because I had a personal investment in a salsa that could be enjoyed without the acid reflux and heartburn—and along the way, I *have* become a millionaire. A multimillionaire, in fact, whose salsa has led to another, much larger business.

Come with me on my journey of turning Asorbas from a money–losing product into a winning financial player. Learn from my mistakes and successes.

CHAPTER 1

MY STORY

"When people realize what you're trying to do and your effort, they will buy your product because of who you are."
—**Duane Thompson**

FAILURE HAS NEVER been an option for me. In the early 2000s, making Asorbas salsa was basically a hobby and I was losing money. But by the end of the decade, there was no more time to play around. I had to make it. The salsa had to succeed.

It was 2009, and I'd just quit a six–figure–income job to focus on my business. I needed to make money, but for an even deeper reason my salsa venture had to bloom and bear fruit. That year, my mother, Patricia Ann Thompson, died at age fifty–seven. Growing up, I'd seen her arrive home physically exhausted and spiritually depleted after long shifts packaging beauty products at a manufacturing warehouse. During the last third or so of her life—after years of attending nursing school at night—she worked as a registered nurse and was far happier workwise than she'd ever been; but even with this achievement, she never really achieved her professional dreams. My mother's passing made me realize that life is about more than working a job you don't love. In fact, I realized I was born to develop and sell my salsa. Yes, I had to succeed.

Mom's death sparked my commitment to make my salsa everything it could be. It provided the ultimate boost to a business journey that had started for me with a problem I had in college . . . and even further back than that.

Many afternoons when I was a kid growing up in Newport News, Virginia, I helped my maternal grandmother, Alma Echoles, plant and tend to vegetables and fruit in a garden she shared with neighbors in our city's downtown. With love, Grandma nurtured her corn, cucumbers, and peach and fig trees. As I worked alongside her, I fell in love with gardening.

Fast-forward many years later when I played football as a defensive lineman for Virginia State University. The team had a tradition of eating chips and salsa after every game. I loved it, but every time I ate the combo, I came down with the worst stomach pain.

After a game freshman year, Grandma emerged from the stands with a care package stocked with roast beef, homemade bread, and victuals from her garden. We'd lost the game, so I'd have to spend the next five hours watching game tapes with the coach and my teammates.

The care package was off-limits. Grandma kissed me goodbye, and I entrusted her gift with my roommate, Eric, to put in the mini-fridge in our dorm room.

Many hours later, exhausted and starving, I walked into my room and into the middle of a party. I smelled roast beef.

"Where's my food?" I asked Eric and a bunch of his friends, who smirked.

The room fell silent. But not for long. I yelled and kicked everyone out, including Eric. I was angry, but I was hungry too. I pulled an illegal hot plate from under my bed and took out of our fridge some red bell peppers, jalapeño peppers, and onions—about the only things left that my grandmother had given me. I added some salt and distilled vinegar, then mixed everything around in the plate and ate the concoction with stale chips. It was *not* good.

The next day, I woke up feeling great. For a minute, I figured there must have been something to the healthy, unprocessed salsa I'd prepared the night before, but I didn't give it more thought than that.

And I didn't make the salsa again—though it made me feel good, like I said, it tasted awful.

So life continued, which means I kept eating a tomato–salsa concoction with unnatural preservatives from the Price Club with my teammates—and I kept having stomach pain. It got so bad, I thought I had an ulcer. Sophomore year, I saw a specialist who checked my acidity level. It was off the charts. His prescription: Quit salsa for a few weeks. My teammates tolerated me breaking the salsa–eating tradition, but after a couple of weeks they urged me to rejoin the eating frenzy. But I didn't want to. For the first time in a long time, my stomach had stopped burning. I wanted to keep feeling good.

The wheels in my head started spinning. That salsa I'd made in my dorm room the year before hadn't had tomatoes, and I wasn't in pain after I'd eaten it. This thought was still turning in my mind a few weeks later during a college nutrition class in which the instructor talked about the benefits of fresh vegetables. After class, I went to the grocery store to buy some vegetables and finally headed to my dorm room, determined to make fresh salsa. I started adding a little bit of this and a little bit of that to my pot, but the main ingredient was diced red bell peppers, which I'd come to learn are less acidic than tomatoes.

For months, as I played around with the salsa recipe in my dorm room, red bell peppers remained a constant ingredient, while other potential ingredients I tested didn't pass muster.

Finally, by junior year, I settled on a mix of the bell peppers, distilled vinegar, red onions, parsley, some tomato, kosher salt, and cilantro. You may be asking, "If tomatoes are so acidic, why did you keep them in the recipe?" Because they added a flavorful zest and the cancer–fighting antioxidant lycopene to the mix. Yes, the antioxidant was a consideration for me even at this young age.

Now, with my ingredient bases more or less covered, I had pretty much perfected the sauce—a medium–hot red bell pepper salsa—and my confidence inspired me to try it out on my teammates. They loved it!

We swapped out the Price Club salsa for my labor of love.

My salsa was born, and so was a dream.

✳✳

Before I get deeper into my story, I have to tell you that I haven't always been great with remembering dates. Pack on top of that the whirlwind years of creating a successful salsa, and things get a little fuzzier still. But what's for sure is that the rest of what I'm about to tell you captures the true spirit of my Asorbas journey . . .

In 1995, with a bachelor's degree in criminal justice from Virginia State, I counseled youth in a juvenile correctional facility in Hanover County, Virginia, and my salsa making went by the wayside. Quickly, I discovered the kids had lots of problems. The job got me down and after a year and a half, I knew I wasn't made for the work.

I was still in my early twenties. I was confused. I didn't know what I wanted to do.

Next, I found myself donning a security guard's uniform at a mall in Richmond, Virginia. The best thing about the job: It paid the bills. Things were going OK, but after just a few months, two women were killed in the mall in a domestic dispute. I watched over a crew that cleaned the blood from the crime scene. I couldn't tolerate the job. I quit.

But I didn't leave the mall. Rodney Eason, the janitorial manager of the mall's housekeeping services, urged me to apply for a position with his division. Within days I was working under him. I took pride in what I did. If I cleaned a toilet, it was the cleanest toilet in the building. Before I knew it, Rodney's supervisor asked me to move into management, and soon I was overseeing housekeeping at a series of malls. A few years into doing this work, I was hired to manage all operations—maintenance, housekeeping, you name it—at Fair Oaks Mall in Fairfax, Virginia.

I did so well in Fairfax that by 1999, I was hired to oversee construction of the million–square–foot Richmond Town Square mall in Richmond Heights, Ohio, and eventually all of its operations. I was making six figures (BIG MONEY!), but after two years I longed for the East Coast again, got married, and moved to Prince George's County, Maryland, to manage office buildings for a real estate management firm. My salary shot up a little more.

Life was good—or so I thought.

**

For a potluck–style holiday party at the Prince George's County job, I broke out my old medium–hot red bell pepper salsa recipe and made a batch. Everything was the same except the vinegar; I swapped in balsamic in place of the distilled because it made the salsa sweeter. Partygoers loved it. One in particular, a convenience/deli store owner who rented space in one of the office buildings I managed, told me he'd sell my salsa if I "bottled" it. So I went to a food store and bought the ingredients and a case of twelve Mason jars. I made twelve labels bearing my face and the name "Duane's Holiday Salsa" on my home computer, put my salsa in the jars, smacked on the labels, then took the jars to his Maryland store. They sold out in two days.

I barely broke even, but right then and there, I caught the salsa–making bug again. It was really more about my ego. It made me feel good knowing the salsa was a hit. In fact, I had to admit that I got a bigger rush from selling it than from my six–figure income. After that first sale, every weekend during my off hours I made Duane's Holiday Salsa at my Upper Marlboro, Maryland, home and delivered it to the store. Soon, I was making it every night at home; I was trying to keep up with consumer demand. In the morning, coworkers wanted to know, "What's that smell in your clothes?" It was the salsa—its essence filled my house. My wife was *not* happy about our aromatic abode.

**

A few years passed, the salsa continued to sell briskly at the convenience store, and I wanted to see if I could sell it elsewhere. I had never made money from it—in fact, I was losing money, because while I had nailed a recipe that had faithful followers, I didn't take the time to price it right. Everything I did was wrong. I was buying my ingredients from regular retail stores—not from wholesalers—and I was breaking the law. Yes, I was unwittingly breaking the law. By making the salsa at home and selling it in a store, with no oversight and unregulated, I could have been fined—or worse. I was determined to take my salsa to the next level though. I was also determined not to make these same mistakes.

I hopped online to learn how to develop a nutritional product and how to put it in the marketplace. I discovered it would have to be professionally tested in a laboratory for factors such as shelf life and calories, and it would have to clear a bunch of federal regulations. I was already beginning to pump my savings pretty liberally into the salsa, so I needed help to cover additional expenses.

Fortunately, a friend came to the rescue. Remember Rodney Eason, my former supervisor with the housekeeping company? In 2004, he loaned me about $5,000 to turn my salsa into a legit product. Rodney's help was the bridge I needed to walk across to get to the next place in the salsa business.

**

With sufficient funding in hand, I sent my product to Kappa Laboratories in Miami. Kappa tested it and found it had a shelf life of eighteen months. I thought this was great. But some months later, I met with Michele Foods Inc. CEO Michele Hoskins, a professional mentor to entrepreneurs in the food–manufacturing business, and learned that eighteen months is not great at all.

The longer the shelf life, the better, Michele said, especially for a new product. It may sit on the shelf longer than well–known products, which could make it more vulnerable to going stale before it's sold, she told me. Michele also advised me to work with a copacker (another way of saying a "manufacturer"), a company that would source my ingredients, cook and package my salsa, and assist with its distribution. At this point, I was still making and bottling the salsa on my own on weekends and weeknights, so if it was going to succeed, I really had to devote the rest of my hours to selling it. I took Michele's advice to heart—I selected a copacker and, in 2006, I incorporated Sabrosa Foods in Virginia to get serious about making sales. By this time, I'd also named my salsa "Sabrosa," which is Spanish for "delicious." I'd change the name to "Asorbas" later.

My copacker, Mama Vida, was based in Randallstown, Maryland, not far from my home. Mama Vida retested my salsa and found that the red onion broke down faster than any other ingredient. They removed it and replaced it with garlic. This simple change extended the salsa's shelf life to two years.

The copacker improved the salsa in other ways too. Not long after I'd had it tested at Kappa, I'd switched from bottling it in twelve–ounce Mason jars to nine–ounce brown jars sealed with black–plastic lids. Some people said the new packaging looked like "hair grease jars." Not only did the salsa suddenly have an image problem, but I found out the hard way that the jars were letting in air.

One day, I opened the back of my truck and heard the *spshw, spshw* before I saw IT: Sauce all over the truck's walls. The jars had exploded. I tried to solve the problem by sealing the lids extra tight, but the tighter they were sealed, the worse the problem became. The plastic lids were bending upward, and there were more explosions.

Mama Vida solved this issue by upgrading the salsa's packaging to a twelve–ounce Mason jar complete with an airtight gold–colored metal lid.

With the salsa's shelf life extended and its image improved, I had a shot at marketing it to big stores. But I had to clear a few other hurdles. I needed the US Department of Agriculture's blessing to offer it legally, a process that would eventually take me a year and a half to complete. And I had other obligations, like obtaining a UPC (Universal Product Code), the number that would identify my product and establish my ownership of it. I paid $800 for a big batch of numbers. Once all of that was done, suddenly my salsa looked like something you'd buy from the grocery store! *Yes!*

Soon, Sabrosa could be found in a few specialty food stores in Virginia.

**

On the weekends, my only free time off from work, I sold Sabrosa in small venues, like farmers' markets, arts and crafts fairs, and even flea markets. And right before people left with a jar, I gave them comment cards I'd picked up from Farm Fresh stores, a supermarket chain in my area. I asked them to write the following on the card:

"Please carry Sabrosa salsa in your store." Then I'd take the cards back from them and mail them to Supervalu, the owner of Farm Fresh and other retail groceries. I mailed Supervalu hundreds of those cards, and then one day corporate called.

Higher–ups at Supervalu wanted to know what all the fuss was about this bell pepper salsa, so they invited me to meet with them. They tasted the product, and in 2007, I signed a contract with a Virginia Beach–based distribution company to put Sabrosa in sixty of their stores, most of them Farm Freshes, across Virginia and in North Carolina.

As all this was taking place, I had divorced and relocated from Maryland to Hampton, Virginia, where I had taken a job overseeing the building of a hospital on Langley Air Force Base. I had made the move to be near my mother, who was dying from pancreatic cancer.

Then March 4, 2009 came. My mother died. The world stopped. Mom's death forced me to take stock of my life. I had cars, houses, and cash, but I wasn't happy. Not only had my marriage ended, but my child—my daughter, Ashley—was not living under my roof.

The day after my bereavement leave ended, I walked into the office at Langley and said, "No more!" I literally left my $160,000 project manager job. I'd had an epiphany: There is more to life than doing things you don't want to do, and there is more to life than making someone else rich. Our days on this Earth are not necessarily many. I was only happy when I was selling salsa. It was time for me to focus on Sabrosa.

The next day I began devoting my daylight time to selling my salsa all over Hampton Roads at swap meets, farmers' markets, $25 tables rented at community yard sales, and other similar venues. This was all while Sabrosa was still being sold at Farm Freshes and smaller retail stores.

I wasn't just selling the salsa. I'd had to put a big chunk of my savings into my business venture, so to keep the lights on at home, I cleaned toilets and waxed and buffed floors at various business locations for a janitorial services company. I did this at night for about a year. I did what I had to do until I could do only what I wanted to do. The job was menial but low stress and part time. It let me live my salsa business. I stayed focused. The strategy worked. By focusing on Sabrosa, today it's my *only* job, and now *I* pay a janitor to keep *my* company's offices clean.

This is what can happen to you when failure is not an option.

**

That's my story—the story I share when people want to know about my product. When I tell them about my journey, they almost always buy my salsa.

So what's your story? What compelled you to make your product or dream about making one? These are important questions, and before we move to the next chapter, write down—in single words, phrases, or a narrative—your answers in the "Thinking Outside the Bottle" section that follows. For example, if I were to write words or phrases to describe my own story, they would be ones like "grandmother," "mother," "acid reflux," "needed a solution to a problem," "loved to cook," "wanted to be happy in my work." It's not too early to figure out the story behind your product. Remember, your product's success will depend on it.

As for the next chapter, here's a preview: As I mentioned in the Introduction, I'll be your mentor on paper (though I'll always urge you to find a real live mentor in your industry). So with that, as your mentor, I'm about to give you your first real *Playbook* lesson—a lesson on *focus*.

Take it from this former defensive lineman: To get anywhere on your product entrepreneur journey, you must keep your eyes on the ball. As you're about to find out in Chapter 2, it's much easier, and you'll have a greater chance of succeeding, if you only have one ball.

THINKING OUTSIDE THE BOTTLE

_____

_____

_____

_____

_____

_____

_____

_____

_____

_____

_____

_____

_____

_____

_____

_____

_____

_____

_____

_____

_____

_____

_____

_____

_____

_____

_____

_____

_____

_____

_____

_____

_____

_____

_____

_____

CHAPTER 2

FOCUS ON ONE PRODUCT: PERFECTING AND CONNECTING

"One product is all you need."—**Duane Thompson**

BEFORE I GET into the nuts and bolts of what it takes to develop and launch a product, I have to say this: If you want to succeed, focus on *one* product, and one product alone. Did I know this when I started selling Asorbas? No! If I'd had the money, I'd probably have produced a bunch of different salsas. Thank goodness I didn't have the money.

I'll give you a couple of real–life examples that will show why you should focus on one product first.

When I started selling Asorbas at fairs and other events, I regularly bumped into another entrepreneur who'd have a table stocked with a dozen different salsas. Meanwhile, I'd be sitting at my table with my one red bell pepper salsa, offered in a medium and mild formulation (I'll go into why I produced a mild version later in this chapter). Time after time, my salsas would sell out or would be close to selling out, while the other seller was left with a bunch of product. Once, a fairgoer who'd visited the other salsa guy's booth then mine, leaned in and told me, "Hmm, your salsa must be good if you only have one."

Here's what was going on: On my display table, I had a bright and simple twelve–inch by twelve–inch sign that listed my product's unique selling attribute: "No acid reflux, no heartburn." People stopped by, curious about the sign. Curiosity turned into a conversation. I'd give them a brief version of my journey to making the salsa, explain how my product worked, and let them sample it. Most of the time, whether the consumer had acid reflux or heartburn issues, they bought the salsa. My sales closure rate was at least 80 percent. People had connected with me and liked what I told them about my product. If I'd had a bunch of different salsas on my table, there's no way I could have listed or talked about the unique selling proposition of them all, and even if I had, I would have still had a problem: Who would have taken the time to read that much material or listen to a long spiel, and especially at a fair or similar event?

Another example: A budding entrepreneur came to my office with about a dozen variety of cakes, all of which he planned to sell. I asked the guy what his story was—why did he make the cakes and what problem did they solve? Well, he didn't have a personal story, and his cakes didn't offer a unique selling point. Even if he'd had a story and his product had solved a problem, he'd have overwhelmed consumers with too many cake options.

The moral of this story is that, no matter how good your product is, if you're just starting out you're far more likely to find success with one product. Here's why:

- **You Can Create a Great Product.** By narrowing your focus, you can create one really great product. Without all the distractions of building, managing, and selling multiple products, you can hone the finer details of your one product and make it much better than any others in the market.

- **You Can Capture a Target Market.** You will fill a niche. Instead of building a product that serves all, you can build a product that serves an underserved market exceptionally well. Target marketing can lead to great success because you can easily capture most of the people who feel underserved. Ultimately, this can mean bigger sales for you.

- **You Can Produce Your Product Quickly.** By targeting one type of consumer, you can rapidly develop your product in the product–testing stages by focusing on one consumer type rather than by splitting your testing efforts between multiple–consumer types. You get to *know* your consumer and become more sensitive to (and cater to) their needs.

- **You Can Build Brand Name Recognition.** When you're just starting out, you're still in the name recognition–seeking game. One product means one product name. Get the buzz going around that name and have it stick on people's tongues and in their minds. You're building a brand, and name recognition is a key part of this process.

Now that the main points have been summarized, let's look at each one as they have applied to Asorbas's success.

Focusing on One Product Allows You to Create the Best Product
By selling one salsa when I started my business, I was able to focus on "perfecting" my salsa. I could take the time to learn which ingredients I needed to eliminate and to add to Asorbas to extend its shelf life. Without the distraction of creating other products, I was also able to *focus*, with the help of Mama Vida, my then–copacker, on making Asorbas's packaging more appealing. As an entrepreneur who was working part time as a janitor to make ends meet, I barely had the financial resources to make my one product a hit, let alone several. If I'd tried to fund several salsas, I probably would have had several failures.

Focusing on One Product Allows You to Capture a Target Market
Early on, I identified Asorbas's target market as consumers who suffer from acid reflux and heartburn, as well as people who like to eat healthy food. By honing the message for these target consumers about the finer attributes of the bell pepper salsa, I created a loyal core of fans in an underserved market. They raved about and bought the salsa.

Focusing on One Product Allows You to Produce It Quickly

Having identified my consumers as people desiring healthy food, I knew just who to offer my salsa to as I was developing it during the testing stages. This helped me quickly determine how it would perform in the marketplace and to move quickly from the testing stage to the actual production stage for real marketplace sales.

Focusing on One Product Allows You to Build Brand Name Recognition

In my first real year in business—when I was no longer selling my salsa at the convenience store—I realized it was more effective to build a brand–recognition campaign around a single product by developing a background story. This allowed me to connect with customers and consumers (I'll address the difference between the two groups in Chapter 4) and eventually the media.

The Beauty of One Product

Because I was only selling a bell pepper salsa, I had time to collect feedback from consumers to continue to make it better. If I'd had additional products to support, I wouldn't have been able to do this as quickly—or at all.

I also had time to develop a lean and stable supply chain that could scale along with my sales growth. I was buying my bell peppers from an established farm on the East Coast for a third of what they would have cost me if I'd bought them from a farm much farther away. And as Sabrosa Foods expanded from a sole proprietorship to a company with several employees, I had time to interview and hire people and to improve the service aspects of my business, such as shipping goods and developing the company website. I am convinced this would not have happened in my company's early stages if I had spent energy and resources developing new products.

So bottom line, if you don't start with a relentless focus on one amazing first product, odds are you won't be a product entrepreneur for long, at least not a successful one. You don't start with the right to do product two. You earn it. Here's how that happened for Asorbas:

During the years I was selling my medium–hot salsa at the arts and crafts fairs and farmers' markets, I met many consumers who don't like even "a hint of hot." They told me they'd love a mild version of my salsa. I wanted to give them what they wanted, so during my first product run with Mama Vida, we produced the medium–hot salsa *and* a mild version—which are considered one product, though each has a slight variance. All the ingredients in the mild salsa are the same as the original's, except it doesn't have jalapeño peppers. After these products sold really well, I later came out with peach chutney and jalapeño pepper relish at the request of loyal consumers. The original medium–hot bell pepper salsa remains the top seller followed by the mild version, but the other products also have their fans. I would never have arrived at the point of producing several well–performing products had I not started out selling just one salsa.

Creating a brand identity within a niche market segment—which is what I did by focusing on one product initially—doesn't demand a revolutionary idea. Your product just needs to have one special thing that separates it from the competition. Concentrate on making it the best solver of a problem, and it should gain recognition.

Take some inspiration from these American companies that built their wealth, at least initially, on one product: Coca–Cola, WD–40, Spanx, Harley–Davidson, and Tabasco hot sauce. And there are more successful American companies out there that did the same. Enough said.

**

Use the "Thinking Outside the Bottle" section that follows to take down any notes or brainstorm ideas related to how your *one* product can serve a target market especially well, how it will be better than its competition, what aspects of the product you need/want to particularly work on to make it stand out, and any other important ideas and notes.

As for our next chapter, we'll look at how to select a name and brand mark for your product and why you should trademark or copyright them. It's a lesson I wish I'd had before I slapped the name "Sabrosa" on jars!

THINKING OUTSIDE THE BOTTLE

_____

_____

_____

_____

_____

_____

_____

_____

_____

_____

_____

_____

_____

_____

_____

_____

_____

_____

_____

_____

_____

_____

_____

_____

_____

_____

_____

_____

_____

_____

_____

_____

_____

CHAPTER 3

BRANDING YOUR PRODUCT: NAMING, TRADEMARKING, AND COPYRIGHTING

"I learned there were other products named 'Sabrosa' in the marketplace. It was time for a name change."
—Duane Thompson

Brand name—The spoken part of a brand's identity (for example, "Asorbas").

Brand mark—The symbol, such as Asorbas's semi–circle encasing a red bell pepper with a left–leaning stem in the middle and crossed at the bottom with a ribbon. A brand mark can also be a sound.

Brand names and brand marks distinguish products from their competitors. They are important because consumers use them to make choices.

**

SELECTING A PRODUCT brand name and mark is serious business and requires care, research, and creativity. In particular, the name should be quick, catchy, intriguing, easy to pronounce, and say something important about what your product delivers. You may want to consult with a branding professional to get pointers on a name as well as your brand mark, an image or even a sound that represents your product—think Nike's swoosh symbol or the tone that may play when you turn on your cell phone.

If you're financially strapped, look for a no–cost route to come up with a brand mark and name—brainstorm ideas and ask professionals, friends, and potential consumers for their opinions. Whatever you're leaning toward, don't fall in love with it too quick. First determine that no other company has a trademark or copyright for the name and mark you want to use. If they've been legally taken, go back to the drawing board and select another name and image.

Don't sell your product without selecting an appropriate brand name and mark and legally protecting them. I speak from experience.

The Sabrosa Brand Mark and Brand Name "Fiascos"

I didn't consult a branding professional or even other people about the brand name and mark I wanted to use. Unfortunately, I learned the hard way how important it is to get outside my own head and bounce ideas off others who are qualified.

First, my brand mark: In my salsa's early years, I just got on the computer and played around with Microsoft Publisher to produce it. It was an image of an "S" engulfed in flames—not exactly smart for a product promoted as the no–heartburn salsa. Consumers were confused over whether the fiery–pictured Sabrosa could really keep heartburn and acid reflux away, but I'd invested too much money in my product's labeling at that point to change it—I'd already paid to copyright it, and too many labels to count had been printed.

As for Asorbas's previous name, Sabrosa, I settled on it after a trip to Trinidad and Tobago with Rodney Eason and later a romantic cruise with my former wife (she was my fiancée at the time) to Cozumel, Mexico. When I heard the word in Trinidad and Tobago, it stuck in my head but didn't get any further than there. I just liked the sound of it. When I heard it during the cruise, I asked the man who had said it—a waiter who called the dish I was eating "sabrosa"—what that meant. He said, "flavorful, delicious." I was sold. So I named my company and my salsa "Sabrosa."

Problem is, there are a ton of products in the world with a similar name, if not the same name. As some years passed, I discovered another salsa and even a strawberry brand called Sabrosa, and several other products with Sabrosa or Sabroso somewhere in the title; and as my salsa's distribution expanded, I began to see that consumers were confusing it with these and other goods.

Then one day I received a cease and desist letter from a company with a product bearing a name similar to Sabrosa's name. This company had trademarked their product's name, and when I researched what it would take to fight off their efforts to force Sabrosa to use a new identifier, I knew that it would not be worth the time or the financial outlay to duke it out in court.

So I had to get creative—something I should have done from the start. I began playing around with "Sabrosa" and came up with "Asorbas"—Sabrosa spelled backward. I thought the name would be fun for my salsa's longtime fans and would refresh the brand campaign for new consumers—plus, too much time had passed for me to reinvent the wheel. The salsa had too many loyal fans, and the new name needed to retain a tie to the old one. I had also researched other brand campaigns and learned that the most successful products have very original names. Asorbas isn't a real word—I knew I'd struck gold. So between the federal government and my lawyer, I paid around $1,800 and spent three months to copyright the name and trademark a new Asorbas brand mark. Since I was changing the name, I used this opportunity to also change the logo to a more appropriate image of a red bell pepper.

Now, no other product can legally use my salsa's name or my symbol. While you won't find Asorbas in the dictionary, and it means nothing, as time wears on it should come to stand for a high–quality, healthy salsa. Who knows, it may find its way into a dictionary one day!

While the salsa's name has changed, my company remains "Sabrosa Foods Inc." because it can. The legal issue isn't with the company name, just the product name—we're branding the product, not the company.

I'm not going to pretend to be any kind of legal expert, so I'll end my discussion here on copyrighting and trademarking. I highly encourage you to contact a lawyer to learn about your options when it comes to legally protecting your product's name and brand mark. And if you believe your product is so unique that it requires a patent, which legally protects your sole right to make and sell your product, then I encourage you to do the same. I have no background in patents—I didn't need a patent to produce Asorbas.

**

Use the "Thinking Outside the Bottle" section to brainstorm product names and images. If you're not artistic, describe the images in words. When thinking up these brand names and marks, consider what your product does, what it delivers, what it conveys, and who you are trying to reach. Write down your responses, then come up with names and images that relate to them.

Remember, the *Playbook* requires you to keep the names quick, catchy, easy to pronounce, yet unique. Think of your personal story and how your product could riff off it. For example, Asorbas could have been called "Alma's" or "Echoles" after my grandmother, who started me on my Asorbas journey. Or I could have named it after my mother, who inspired me to leave my well–paying job to make a real go of it as a product entrepreneur.

After you have drawn up your list, check to see what's on it that may have already been trademarked or copyrighted. Keep pushing.

You don't have to select your product's name and mark before you sit down to create your business plan, but you should have a list of potential names and images drawn up by then. It's good to have solid ideas of what the name and mark could be by the time you contact a lawyer, who you should identify in your plan, which we'll cover in the next chapter.

THINKING OUTSIDE THE BOTTLE

_____

_____

_____

_____

_____

_____

_____

_____

_____

_____

_____

_____

_____

_____

_____

_____

_____

_____

_____

_____

_____

_____

_____

_____

_____

_____

_____

_____

_____

_____

_____

_____

_____

CHAPTER 4

THE BUSINESS PLAN: YOUR MAP TO SUCCESS

"To keep going, you must recognize the relativity of your achievement."
—Duane Thompson

NOW THAT YOU'RE going to create just one product and you have or are on your way to selecting a brand name and mark, you need to create a business plan. You need to write it down before you even think about "perfecting" your product. You know that when I started out I had no plan. I was just making salsa, selling it at my friend's convenience store, and losing money. Had I taken the time to figure out some basic logistics, I'm sure I would have made *some* money—not much, granted, since I was operating at such a small level at the time—but I wouldn't have *lost* money.

The point: No matter how small your operation is, *always* put a business plan in motion before you start doing business. You need to follow a roadmap to ensure you'll hit your planned destination: Sales Success. It is not enough just to develop a good product and have a great story behind it. You must develop a workable business model too.

This finally got through my head after I got serious about selling my salsa. I began to draw from many of the ideas and practices I had picked up during my years managing and overseeing operations for large buildings—in those arenas, we always had business plans, so why shouldn't I as a small businessperson? I'll go into more detail about this in Chapter 11, where I talk about the skillsets you may already possess that can help you succeed in business.

Before we begin the work of creating a business plan, however, there are two things I'm going to address in–depth because they will come up in the language and ideas you use in your plan and in this book over and over:

1) Don't confuse your "customer" with the "consumer," and 2) Don't confuse yourself with your consumer.

- **Confusing the Customer with the Consumer.** Most people think the words *customer* and *consumer* are interchangeable. They are not. As a businessperson, get into the habit of seeing the stores and other venues you'll sell your product through, as well as the distributor or brokers you'll work with, as your *customers*. For example, for Asorbas, in the early days my customers included Farm Fresh and Mama Vida. The *consumer*, on the other hand, is the individual who walks into a store to purchase your product or who purchases it online.

  Always remember that customers and consumers see a product very differently. Let's start with the *customer*:

  The *customer* buys your product or works with you to produce your product to address a business requirement. The customer has very different concerns than the people who use your product every day. Your product has to make business sense to your customer—how will selling it, manufacturing it, distributing it, serving as your broker, etc., help them boost their bottom line? For example, if your product is a doll, would it make sense to try to get it onto the shelves of a grocery store? It may. In particular, I'm thinking of a Hampton Roads, Virginia–area grocery store that sells a handful of Barbies a few aisles down from the cereals and breads. The store is nestled in a community of luxury–apartment renters with small children and established families living in elegant homes. Apparently, the product makes sense to the store given the demographic profile of the surrounding community. The moral of this story: As you're putting together your business plan, do your research and figure out what your customer sells and what they *don't* sell, but possibly could sell successfully. Investigate the obvious opportunities, but don't overlook the less obvious ones.

As for your *consumers*—the people buying your product—you also need to research them. Too often the entrepreneur is only exposed to the buyers or economic decision makers who try to represent the needs of the consumers; but you can't stop there. It is critical to have a clear understanding of the different types of people who will actually use the product. Break them down into the various demographic groups that would influence a purchase of the product like the one you're selling. If you're a crystal vase maker, for example, who are you marketing your vases to—young children, young adults, seniors? It's fair to say that you won't be selling your product to kids, which means adults with young kids may not have a big interest in your vases either. They may like the idea of having vases to beautify their home, but in their mind this image will be quickly replaced by one of their child running around the house, knocking into the dining room table, and the vase hurtling to the hardwood floor. They will not be a consumer of your product.

Now that we've clarified the difference between the *customer* and *consumer*, let's look at why it's important to *not confuse yourself with the consumer*.

Often, entrepreneurs think of themselves as their target consumer. This can be a dangerous pitfall. There are many negative consequences of this confusion, and the most common one is an unusable product. For example, you may be able to use your product with ease, yet the actual target consumer, who is not immersed in the world of similar products, may find it complicated and overwhelming. You must constantly put your product in front of consumers from your target demographic and carefully consider their responses. Don't take shortcuts.

Now that you understand why you shouldn't confuse yourself with your target consumer, we're ready to look at what your business plan should entail—the "must–dos." It's time to break out the Sticky Notes and highlighters!

The Must–Dos of a Great Business Plan

Business plans are made, not born. Focus on:

Business Support Team

- Describe the type of business mentor(s) you need and how you will find that mentor (or mentors). This is the first must–do on the list because it's one of the most important things in your business plan. I wish I had had business owner and mentor Michele Hoskins in my life much sooner, because Asorbas would have gotten farther faster.

  Ideally, you'll want a mentor who has successfully launched a product in a product category similar to your own. For instance, while Michele doesn't produce salsa, she does produce a food product, so she was able to give me relevant advice about what it would take to launch and run a food–based product business.

  As for how I found Michele, I got lucky. A friend of mine met her at a conference, picked up her business card and later gave it to me. The rest is history.

  As for you, potential ways to find a mentor or mentors could include: attending conferences, fairs, entrepreneur incubators, and trade events; going online; getting references from other professionals and former colleagues; and tapping into your university or college alma mater.

- Join respective industry trade groups and clubs to find collegial support from other entrepreneurs. For instance, I got involved with a local club for pepper lovers and a local group of entrepreneurs. These groups helped me become a better bell pepper salsa maker!

Product Development

- Describe your product and its unique selling point (in my case, a healthy salsa based with red bell peppers to help stave off acid reflux and heartburn).

- Describe your product's mission. For example, Sabrosa Foods's mission is to "provide healthy all–natural gourmet condiments."

- Devise an experiment to test your product so that you can refine it before bringing it to the market. (I go into detail about this in the next chapter, "The Product Development Playbook.")

- Identify appropriate trade shows and events where you can promote and sell your product to receive unbiased feedback during its development (and later, simply to sell when it's finished). Remember, the Internet is your friend, and you can use it to find these opportunities.

- Familiarize yourself with state and federal laws addressing your product, and determine when and how you will comply with them. I discovered that the Food and Drug Administration requires you must be certified to produce acidified foods, so I took a week–and–a–half–long course to meet their requirement.

Competitive Analysis

- Identify your competition. Find them online, in your local Yellow Pages, in commercial venues where their product is sold, and through word of mouth.

- Describe your competition, what makes you different from them, and how you can provide a better product than they do. Here's a page from my own business plan:

Sabrosa Foods Inc.'s competitive advantage will be to provide healthy, great–tasting high–end gourmet condiment substitutes. Sabrosa Foods believes it will achieve this goal and be better than its competition. In addition to staying on top of changing consumer preferences and being successful in the long run, Sabrosa Foods will constantly look for ways to cut costs and increase productivity while still making a profit.

Market Analysis

- Describe and analyze your potential market: Who will your consumers be? How many people will you be serving? Where will they be located? What will they be willing to pay? For example, I determined that my consumers would be salsa lovers who suffer from acid reflux and heartburn as well as consumers who prefer healthier food options, which, in food– business lingo, are specialty food items. This is what I stated in my business plan:

The current products of Sabrosa Foods satisfy the very active, health–conscious consumers in the specialty food industry because we provide high–quality ingredients, which makes for a better quality product. This consumer pays more for a specialty food item because the quality of the ingredients justifies the higher price.

Further, my plan provided an analysis of the market I was entering and offered proof that my salsa would be sold in a growth industry:

Between 2000 and 2005, the private–label gourmet condiment market grew at an annual rate of 5.3 percent, with the $85 billion food segment accounting for the strongest increase. By 2010, the market value of private–label food alone is expected to surpass $100 billion, according to Datamonitor. The Private Label Manufacturers Association recently released AC Nielsen findings stating that private–label sales outpaced branded sales two–to–one over the past seven years.

Today's more informed consumer expects private–label products to be of better quality. Private labels represent a choice and an opportunity to purchase quality products at varying price points. Specialized flavor profiles can make a consumer "trade up" in dollars while establishing brand loyalty, which contributes to repeat business and a better bottom line for the retailer.

Marketing Strategy

- Have a marketing strategy: How will you get the word out about your product? Will it be through paid advertising, and if so, what avenue will make the most sense to pursue—radio, TV, magazines, newspapers, websites, or will you pursue free advertising through social media or by way of free features on radio, TV, in magazines, newspapers, or online? (I will go into detail about how I marketed my salsa in Chapter 8, "Don't Pay for Advertising When the Media Will Do It for Free." I highly recommend free whenever you can get it!)

- Familiarize yourself with local marketing strategies offered by your municipality. For example, your city may offer free website development (or tax deferments, for that matter) if you open a business there.

Operations and Management

- Describe your potential business location: Where will your office be located? Will you work on developing your product in the same place you work on day–to–day business tasks (making phone calls, keeping track of bills, etc.)? If not, where will your product development lab be located?

- Devise an operations plan. Ultimately, where will your finished product be made? Remember, you need to find the right customer to do business with to give your product a shot at succeeding. Answer these questions: Who will you employ to manufacture it? Who will you employ to distribute it? Find out who are the best manufacturers of your product type, then seek them out and conduct one–on–one interviews to see if they're a good fit for you financially and otherwise. (This topic will be further detailed in Chapter 6.) Look up potential manufacturers, distributors, and brokers on the Internet by searching terms like "product manufacturers," "product distributors," and "product brokers," and by plugging in your product category name in the search engine. For instance, I would plug in "food," whereas an entrepreneur with a car–related product, for example, might plug in "car," "vehicle," or "transportation."

- Identify professionals and resources you will need now and down the road. This includes accountants, lawyers, and other seasoned professionals. Look them up on the Internet, talk to other product entrepreneurs, find them in magazines devoted to entrepreneurs, and go to conferences. You don't know it all, and you need to surround yourself with experts. You will need professionals in your life before you need or can afford employees.

- Set an estimated time when you will hire employees. If you're like many entrepreneurs, you don't have the resources to do this now, but if your business takes off, that time will come.

- Schedule meet–and–greets with an accountant and lawyer to learn how to set up your business. Check to see if they offer free initial consultations. You don't want to inadvertently break tax laws or violate regulations. The lawyer may also provide some low–cost or free information on the business–name trademarking and copyrighting processes in addition to other legal issues.

Financial Factors

- Analyze the potential risks and problems associated with launching and selling your product. In my plan I noted that the economy could stumble and gourmet–food consumers might scale back their purchases. A couple of other potential risks I addressed: *Company is unable to keep up with changing factors in the targeted segments* and *Constant entry of new competitors with more capital may win any potential market share.*

- Analyze your product's potential financials. You need to consider how much money it will take to produce it and how much you'll need to charge for it to get a return on investment.

- Analyze how you will raise the money to produce your product. For example, I worked with friends and family and used my savings. Other potential sources of capital include, but are certainly not limited to: a loan from the Small Business Administration or your bank; an angel investor—a very wealthy professional or entrepreneur; and crowdfunding—typically, this is the process of raising money from large groups of people on the Internet. Look into the pros and cons of all these options and research other ways to raise funds.

- Account for product liability insurance. Find the best carrier for your product and buy their plan.

Future Possibilities

- Visualize your product in five years, ten years, and fifteen years. At each of these phases, where do you see your product? Is it being sold in thousands of stores across the US? Online only? Have you sold your product to another company so that you can bask in the sunshine work–free on the beautiful beaches of Hawaii?

Business Plan Executive Summary

Now that we've covered what your business plan should entail, let's look at the executive summary of the business plan I devised in 2009. This summary should highlight your plan's main ideas and objectives. It should be one of the first pages in your plan. Note how my summary encompasses most of the must–dos on the preceding checklist:

Sabrosa Foods is a food manufacturer in the specialty foods industry and sells its products on a wholesale basis to brokers, distributors, and retailers. The goal of the company is to produce and sell for a profit gourmet specialty foods. The company's mission is to provide healthy all–natural gourmet condiments. The product is an all–natural no preservatives roasted bell pepper salsa, packaged in a twelve–ounce jar in both mild and medium heat levels. The product is a rich–textured homestyle roasted salsa that sustains the individual flavors of the all–natural ingredients of roasted red bell peppers, garlic, cilantro, roasted jalapeño peppers, diced tomatoes, sea salt, and balsamic vinegar.

Sabrosa Foods utilizes a copacker for processing purposes. A copacker is a company that has the facilities to process foods for public consumption. In order to be an acceptable and legitimate copacker, the company must be certified by the Food and Drug Administration and the Department of Health for their respective regions. Sabrosa Foods's copacker is Mama Vida Inc., located in Randallstown, Maryland. Taking marginal costs and operating *expenses into consideration along with primary competition prices, Sabrosa Foods salsa's wholesale cost is $3. The company's primary competition has its product priced at $2.99 on the wholesale level.*

Sabrosa Foods's salsa will be found at three concept stores: grade "A" grocery stores, specialty food stores, and gift shops. Sabrosa Foods will utilize mostly push strategy efforts through the use of guerrilla–marketing tactics. The types of sale promotions utilized are trade oriented in the form of credit terms, discount offers, and occasional volume discounts. Consumer–oriented sales promotions will be through print media, such as point of purchase recipes and some couponing (premiums).

Sabrosa Foods's immediate mission is to earn a position in consumers' minds as a manufacturer of high–quality foods in the specialty foods industry. The company will do this by producing products that have an authentic texture and flavor by using the highest quality ingredients possible. Objectives are to be positioned in the specialty foods market throughout the United States by 2010 with sales volume increasing 12% on an annual basis. These figures will be based on the number of case units sold annually (12/12 oz. pack).

To successfully sell the products, an estimated working capital of $50,000 will be required to produce, warehouse, market, advertise, and run the daily operation. The return on investment with market interest is anticipated to start six to twelve months after the initial draw and expected to be paid in full after forty–eight months.

Now, let's take a more detailed look at my plan's marketing strategy section. You'll understand why we're doing this when you arrive near the end of this chapter. Notice the in–depth descriptions of where and when I planned to sell the salsa.

Sabrosa Foods Inc.'s marketing strategy is based on serving niche gourmet food markets. The world is full of consumers who can't get what they perceive to be high–quality or authentic products. The company will capitalize both on the "Pure Flavor Sabrosa Tradition" and "Healthy Aspects" in their product line. Furthermore, Sabrosa Foods is focused on building a marketing infrastructure that will provide what appears to be a seamless approach to their products, covering multiple avenues by utilizing grocery stores and major distributors. Each location will accent the other, providing for continuous exposure of the Sabrosa brand. Sabrosa Foods has characterized the following marketing segments for prospecting and distribution:

1. *Hampton Roads, Segment 1—slated to be the first introduction segment for Sabrosa Foods Inc. flagship salsa products, this segment consists of seven Virginia cities—Hampton, Newport News, Portsmouth, Virginia Beach, Chesapeake, Suffolk, and Norfolk—with a population of more than 1.6 million. This segment grew at a 1.17% annual rate from 1990 to 2000. Hampton Roads is the 31st largest metropolitan/consolidated statistical area in the nation. Its effective buying power (EBI) according to Sales, Marketing and Management is more than $20.8 billion.*

2. *Richmond, Segment 2—Richmond, Virginia was chosen as the second segment by Sabrosa Foods because of the large availability of specialty retail markets, seasonal outdoor farmers' markets, and gourmet grocery stores. The city is considered a metropolitan area and has a population of approximately 197,000. It is broken out into seven regions— South Side, South West, West End, Central, Downtown, East End, and North Side. Richmond also has surrounding counties: Chesterfield County, Hanover County, Henrico County, and New Kent County, all of which are ideal for branch marketing*

once distribution is established. This segment is anticipated to be addressed as soon as segment 1 is stabilized.

3. *Delmarva, Segment 3—This segment consists of Northern Virginia, Washington DC, Maryland, and Delaware and is by far the largest segment of the three chosen by Sabrosa Foods. This segment is anticipated to be a challenge just on the fact that each entity is a state with the exception of Washington, DC. This combined segment has a population of approximately 8 million and is host to some of the nation's most recognized specialty retailers.*

4. *Festivals and Events—Sabrosa Foods will utilize this method as a tactical marketing tool to promote their products as well as to bring in ancillary sales to add to the company's bottom line.*

Meeting Business Plan Objectives

I came pretty darn close to meeting all of the objectives in my original business plan. I was off on the timing, though—things didn't always happen when I had projected they would, but the point is, good things did eventually happen.

Remember, business plans are living documents. You have to adjust as you go. Periodically review your plan against how your business is performing, and then adjust and repeat.

A Parting Word about Meeting Your Expectations

I didn't get discouraged or think of giving up on my salsa venture when I didn't meet my goals when I had planned. That's because I knew I was still making progress, however slow. I knew where the bottom had been. I remembered well the days of making no money selling Duane's Holiday Salsa at the convenience store versus the slow–but–steady progress toward becoming the guy with a profit–making salsa sold in well–known stores around Virginia and North Carolina . . . and eventually elsewhere.

In short, I recognized the relativity of my achievement. I had not met all my goals, but in terms of store placement, sales, and brand recognition, Asorbas was galaxies ahead of the days when it was sold in the convenience store.

If you're going to succeed, you have to be persistent and have vision—an essential *Playbook* rule. Remember one of the must-dos for your business plan was writing out your vision of where you see your product in five, ten, and fifteen years? You'll only get to these milestones if you keep pushing.

Always keep in mind, business has a way of self-correcting if you give it the room it needs.

**

Use "Thinking Outside the Bottle" to address your business plan must-dos. Because there is so much ground to cover, you'll have a few extra pages in this section to write notes. Meanwhile, stay excited about what's coming in the next chapter—"The Product Development Playbook" will show you how to create and finalize your product.

THINKING OUTSIDE THE BOTTLE

_____

_____

_____

_____

_____

_____

_____

_____

_____

_____

_____

_____

_____

_____

_____

_____

_____

_____

_____

_____

_____

_____

_____

_____

_____

_____

_____

_____

_____

_____

_____

_____

_____

_____

_____

_____

_____

_____

_____

_____

_____

_____

_____

_____

_____

CHAPTER 5

THE PRODUCT DEVELOPMENT PLAYBOOK: DEVELOPING, TESTING, AND MEASURING TO PRODUCE "PERFECTION"

*"Whatever you build, you want it to be sustainable
and appeal to a specific audience so
they'll want to use it again and again."*
—Duane Thompson

WHETHER YOU'RE CREATING a book, toy, food, tool, mode of transport, clothing—in short, any type of product—you must adequately develop it, test it, and measure its performance before you bring it to the marketplace.

This takes patience and perseverance. If ever you find yourself frustrated by the time it's taking to get your product right, think of the Wright Brothers, Wilbur and Orville, who are credited with creating the first successful airplane.

The brothers spent four years manipulating the components of a glider before finally installing a propeller and engine into their design to test whether it could truly fly. Their first powered–flight attempt, in Kitty Hawk, North Carolina, on December 14, 1903, lasted all of three seconds, with the glider becoming airborne before crashing into the sand. Then, on December 17 of that same year, they made their next attempt. The glider flew for twelve seconds over a distance of 120 feet. As the day wore on and they continued to test, their machine's performance improved, traveling as far as 852 feet over fifty–nine seconds. Of course, the product underwent many, many more tests and improvements . . . and the Wright Brothers went down in history.

The airplane is definitely a product that changed lives. Now an airplane can travel all around the world.

Thanks, Wilbur and Orville, for providing a model of perseverance.

To succeed, you must stay the course like the Wrights. Also, you must approach product development with the attitude that you'll be happy with your final product—provided your customers and consumers are happy with it. This seems obvious, but it may not be if this is the first time you've created anything. The simple truth is, many times the product you envisioned and planned does not match up, at least not entirely, to the final product you produce. This was true for my salsa.

After I tasted the first salsa batch Mama Vida made, I was speechless. It didn't compare to what I'd been making and selling for years, despite the fact the ingredients in the medium–hot bell pepper salsa, save for the garlic that was swapped in for the red onion, were the same.

Quickly, I discovered Mama Vida's mixing and cooking methods were entirely different from my own. And because they were producing enormous batches, they couldn't use what I had—all farmers' market and natural food store ingredients. Mama Vida *did* use fresh ingredients, however, but they completed the recipe with canned tomatoes. They had to do that to improve the product's bottom line. Consequently, my salsa had to be royally tweaked to come close to matching the salsa I was accustomed to making in my home kitchen; but with persistence and motivation, Mama Vida and I came up with a taste and consistency that worked. However, the salsa on shelves today still does not taste the same as the one I made in my kitchen years ago, nor will it ever. But customers and consumers like the product, so I am satisfied with the commercial version we sell now.

That's my story. Yours may be different. Once your final product emerges, it may be stronger than what you originally produced or dreamed. Keep an open mind about what will constitute success. That's imperative as you engage in product development. Remember, you're not necessarily failing if your product doesn't meet your original standard—in fact, you may be succeeding.

Product Development Steps

Now, we're going to examine the critical steps of product development. I'm going to assume your product is in the preliminary stages of getting off the ground—that it's where Asorbas was when I pulled it from my friend's convenience store to sell it to the world at large: You have a viable product, but it hasn't been fully developed and tested, and depending on the type of product, you're not yet in a position to legally sell it. (By the way, by this point you should have already selected your manufacturer. Choosing a manufacturer is so important, it is treated fully in the next chapter.)

How you develop your product may differ from an entrepreneur whose product is not similar to yours, but many of the basics of product development apply across the board regardless of product type. Let's examine the product development steps.

Developing, Testing, and Measuring for Product "Perfection"

Step One: Develop Your Story

Before you test your product on consumers, you must start developing your story. That's right—develop your story, your product's story. In Chapter 1, I shared my story—the story behind Asorbas—and charged you with brainstorming words or phrases that answer the question, "What compelled you to make your product or dream about making one?" Your answer should be compelling, engaging, and honest. Now that you have your phrases and words, put together a verbal narrative—the personal story behind your product. Share it with your husband, wife, partner, significant other, friends, parents, children, the bartender, massage therapist, beautician, barber. Refine your story. Adjust and repeat. Repeat it at trade shows and other venues where you may initially sell your product. See how it plays. Do people want to hear more? Did they engage with you because of it? Did it help you sell the product? Get your story down.

Write Your Story:

_____

_____

_____

_____

_____

_____

_____

_____

_____

_____

_____

Step Two: Determine Your Potential Market's Demographics

Determine the demographics of your product's market: Who is going to buy your product? How many potential consumers fit into this niche? You have a slew of questions to answer here:

- Where do your consumers live (city, county, particular part of town)?
- What is the age range of your potential consumers?
- Are your consumers male or female or both?
- What is their income level?
- What is their education level?
- Where do they fit on the career scale—are they white or blue collar?
- Are your consumers married or single?
- Do they have children?
- Do they have a pet?
- What are their typical hobbies and interests?
- What are their religious and political traits?
- Do your potential consumers know they need this product?
- Where do your consumers hang out on the Internet?

Answer the Questions:

_____

_____

_____

_____

_____

_____

_____

_____

_____

_____

_____

_____

_____

Step Three: Test Your Product on Your Market

It is crucial to understand how consumers perceive your product, so you need to find out how they respond to it. Design and execute a fast, inexpensive experiment to test your product on your target market, then analyze the results and feedback. These small experiments should be performed until you completely understand the demographic you're targeting your product to and all the benefits your product offers to this demographic. Each experiment should lead to greater understanding about how to better match up what people need with what the product delivers.

Here's how I tested my salsa:

I first developed a concept of how a roasted low–acidic red bell pepper salsa brought value to the person eating it. My concept, which became my product's tagline, was that Asorbas (again, called "Sabrosa" back in those days, though I choose to use its current name) is a "no heartburn" and "no acid reflux" salsa that you can enjoy without worries.

I had formulated a consumer problem/solution scenario based on the research of my potential market (performed in Step Two), that led me to define Asorbas's target end–user—the *consumer*—as people who simply like healthy foods as well as those who suffer from acid reflux or heartburn. I knew I had a sizable market for my salsa after researching the Internet and seeing the craze for healthy foods as well as the gazillions of dollars Proctor & Gamble's Pepto–Bismol, which helps relieve heartburn and other ailments, was raking in. It made sense to sell people on the idea of enjoying a salsa without worrying about having a burning tummy or throat. In my gut, I knew I had created a product that people would want.

Having identified my core consumer, next I designed a market test that would involve putting my salsa in front of two test groups: people offered a salsa boasting "no acid reflux" and "no heartburn" and people offered a salsa under a banner stating "Try this Island–Style 7–Ingredient Salsa." The information I gathered from these groups would help me confirm or deny my product's selling potential with the acid reflux, heartburn sufferers' group.

Next, I clearly defined the problem my salsa would solve from a consumer's perspective. I focused on consumer–phrase solutions like, "If you're like me, most tomato–based salsas keep you up at night," and sayings from a business point of view like, "Consumers are looking to eat healthier and understand the effects of better ingredients." I now had the proposition I'd put before the test group encountering the no acid reflux/no heartburn sign: "Consumers have problems finding great–tasting condiments made from natural ingredients without causing acid reflux or heartburn. (This salsa) will solve that problem: It's the 'no heartburn, no acid reflux' salsa they've been dreaming of." The other group hearing only "Try this Island–Style 7–Ingredient Salsa" would be the control group.

I found a group of approximately 200–300 potential consumers fitting my potential consumer demographic. I split the group in half: 150 consumers would receive the "No Acid Reflux," "No Heartburn" offer while the other half would get the "Island–Style Salsa" offer. To avoid cross marketing, I ran this test for one summer using two outdoor farmers' markets located on opposite ends of town. Once the campaign was over, I measured its effectiveness by comparing the revenue of one group to the other.

Hands down, when the salsa was advertised as a no–acid–reflux, no–heartburn formulation, people bought it at a rate more than double of that when it was advertised as Try Island Style. This confirmed I needed to heavily promote the salsa to consumers looking for healthier fare *and* to the acid reflux/heartburn crowd. Another interesting note: I was also testing product prices on consumers at this point. Sales were good at $7, but they fell when I put a higher price on the salsa. So around $7 was the sweet spot, and I stuck with that.

Design Your Market Test:

_____

_____

_____

_____

_____

_____

_____

_____

_____

_____

Step Four: Design Secure Packaging

Your product is more than just the item *inside* the jar or the box; it's also the jar or the box itself. Remember how those first Sabrosa Foods jars exploded on me? Good thing the salsa was in the development phase. After we identified the problem, Mama Vida came up with a better solution for the jars, and the rest is history.

In the case of many, though not all, products, there are some specific things you must do before you can finalize your packaging. For instance, certain products must meet specific industry–size requirements. Once you determine what those are, you must also consult applicable regulations to determine whether your product should be sold by units, weights, or volume.

Finally, you must carefully select the material you use to create your packaging to ensure it adequately protects your product, and, if there are packaging requirements, helps your product meet the requirements. Depending on your product, you may have a number of choices:

Metals—Advantages: inexpensive, nontoxic, strong. Disadvantages: steel must be coated with tin, chromium, or various polymers for acidic foods; aluminum is sensitive to chloride ions and acidic foods.

Glass—Advantages: nonreactive, impervious to moisture and gases, see–through, recyclable. Disadvantages: extremely fragile, very heavy.

Paper—Advantages: lightweight, generally inexpensive, excellent surface for printing. Disadvantages: becomes weaker when wet, restricted to certain applications when used alone.

Plastics—Advantages: resistant to breakage, relatively inexpensive, corrosion resistant, lightweight, waterproof. Disadvantages: bends, crushes, or cracks easily, some possess little heat resistance, easily picks up dust.

Laminates—Advantages: combines the advantages of several materials into one. Disadvantages: can be more costly than plastics.

Potential Product Packaging Materials:

_____

_____

_____

_____

_____

_____

_____

_____

**Step Five: Design Attractive Packaging—People DO Choose
a Book by Its Cover**

You might have the best and most securely packed product in the
world, but if it comes in an unattractive or confusing package you may
lose the sales game right there. Remember, my salsa was once sold in
what some people told me looked like "hair grease" jars.

Fact is, one of the greatest influences on people's decision to buy a
product is the package it comes in. Some products, of course, aren't in
a package per se—think cars, most furniture, and clothes. Realize that
if you have a product similar to these, your product *is* its own package.
One of the most famous examples of this is the classic Coca–Cola
bottle: Its gorgeous curvaceous shape is a registered trademark, and

once you see that silhouette, you know you're looking at a bottle of Coke. On the flip side, consider this example: You may have invented the most comfortable office chair ever, but if it is the most hideous chair ever, you'll probably have a tough time selling it. Always remember the Coca–Cola model, and you can't go wrong.

Product Packaging Image Ideas:

_____

_____

_____

_____

_____

_____

_____

_____

_____

Step Six: Obtain a Unique Product Code
The product you make will determine the type of unique code it will require. For example, books have what is called an ISBN (International Standard Business Number) and food products and many other products have a UPC (Universal Product Code). These codes and numbers serve as the Social Security number, so to speak, for a product—no two are

alike. Not only do they identify your product, helping, for example, a retailer keep track of its sales, but they also establish your ownership of it.

Buy your product's unique code/number from the source that produces that number—not from the manufacturer (or anyone else) you'll be working with to produce the product.

Plans for Obtaining Your Unique Product Code:

_____

_____

_____

_____

_____

Step Seven: Create Your Product Label

A label is an information tag, wrapper, seal, or imprinted message attached to a product. It informs consumers about a product's contents and gives directions. For instance, a cake–mix box may explain how many eggs and other added ingredients are required to use in the mix. The label is also where your product's unique code will appear. If your product is a book, your code will appear on the back cover.

Label Types
- Brand Label—gives the product's brand name (By this point you should have tested, or be in the process of testing, brand names and marks on professionals and consumers.)
- Descriptive Label—informs about product use, care, other features
- Grade Label—states the product quality

Labeling Laws

- Be aware that many package labels must meet local, state, and federal standards. Consider the following:
- Food and Drug Administration (FDA)—This agency regulates health claims. If you're claiming your product helps improve a health problem, for example, it better do exactly what you say it does or you'll be in hot water with the FDA.
- Federal Trade Commission (FTC)—The FTC monitors deceptive advertising. Be sure you're accurately representing your product to avoid getting in trouble with the commission.

Product Label Components

- Color—Choose attractive color combinations that do not clash.
- Graphics—Use eye–catching graphics to draw attention to the product.
- Readability—Make sure the label is readable at a glance. Typically, you have two to three seconds to attract a consumer's attention. Include a brand logo, company name, and two or three words describing the product in type that can be read from six feet away.
- Fonts—Use good–looking, easy–to–read fonts.
- Material—Your label material should fit the idea of the product. For example, for a product with a natural theme, you could use a textured paper that conveys a handcrafted look.
- Label Finish—Whether you choose a glossy or matte finish depends on the kind of image you want to convey. A matte laminate can provide a classier look that's easy to read, whereas gloss will add some impact to the colors on the label and provide a shiny, reflective look.
- Label Size and Shapes—Draw attention to labels by using unusual label shapes.
- Keep a Consistent Theme—It is important to keep major design elements of your label consistent. For example, whether

a consumer is looking at Asorbas's bell pepper, jalapeño, or peach flavors, they recognize instantly that it comes from the same company and brand.

- Contact Information—Every company should have contact information on product labels.

A quick word about working with graphics designers: I always approached them with several ideas for my labels. The designer would take my suggestions and bring them to life in a way that only a professional artist can. But getting to that point didn't come easy. The first few designers I worked with didn't turn around logos and labels that worked for me. I burned through several designers for this very reason. This was mostly my fault. I hadn't been communicating my vision and needs well; this is a skill I've since developed. Make sure you tell the designer *exactly* how you want your label and logo to look.

Label Notes:

_____

_____

_____

_____

_____

_____

_____

Step Eight: Produce a Prototype

Now that you have put your product through steps one through seven, it's time to create your prototype. Ideally, this is where your manufacturer would first come in—if you have the financial means, you'll pay the manufacturer to produce samples. Put your product in its new packaging and head out with it and your product story into the world.

Go back to your potential target–market consumer to sample your prototype and ask if they would buy it and if so, how much they would pay for it. If they criticize your product, ask how they think it could be improved.

Compare your product with similar products and continually ask, "Why would someone switch and buy from me?" Solicit negative opinions. Don't fall in love with your idea—be an optimistic pessimist by always looking for the flaws in your product and ways to improve its consumer perception.

During this phase, you should be participating in trade shows and exhibitions for real–time feedback. Walk the floor to look for products that are similar to yours. Talk with product buyers—sophisticated buyers at trade shows know immediately whether your product has a chance at succeeding.

If your results during this stage are largely negative—poor sales, consumer complaints, no tradeshow interest—you should consider abandoning your idea or reconfiguring it.

Prototype Notes:

_____

_____

_____

_____

_____

_____

_____

_____

_____

_____

_____

_____

_____

Step Nine: Continuous Improvement

While you're putting your product through steps one through eight, you must continuously improve it. Before you take it to store shelves, you MUST continue to enlist testers, unbiased people who will try out your product for flaws and provide feedback on its packaging and other features. A few trips to the trade shows and exhibitions are not enough. Keep making the rounds and find other venues where you can test it out. If your product is a book, refine it through further edits or rewrites after passing it by and getting the advice of qualified readers. You can also provide several examples of book cover art online, or you can create several physical prototype covers and survey readers on their favorite cover. If your product is an educational toy, see if a teacher in your local school system would be willing to share it with students and allow you to sit in on their play session to take notes. If it's a food product, try it out on people at fairs and farmers' markets, like I did. Ask them what they like or don't like about your product, from its taste to its packaging. Make appropriate improvements.

Continuous Improvement Notes:

_____

_____

_____

_____

_____

_____

_____

_____

_____

_____

_____

_____

Step Ten: Get Your Manufacturer's Take on Your Prototype
Take your continuous improvement notes to your manufacturer. Have them make another test batch of your product according to your specifications and see how the real thing looks, feels, reads, tastes. Are the book's pages too thin, the type too small? Will the soup last on the shelf two years or only a year and a half? Did switching the type of fabric you're using to produce your pillows make them rough? Take notes, make improvements, adjust and repeat.

Additional Prototype Notes:

_____

_____

_____

_____

_____

_____

_____

_____

_____

_____

Step Eleven: Determine Your Product Cost
You must know what it costs to produce your product. *Product cost* is what *you* pay to make a single unit of product.

The following steps will show you how to determine your product cost and, ultimately, your product's *sales price*, what the *consumer* pays at the cash register, to help you achieve maximum profit.

How to Determine Your Product Cost

1) Create a List of Product Components

Determine what components you need to produce each unit of your product (for Asorbas, one unit of product is one jar of salsa). Consider everything you need, both *hard (material) costs* and *soft (service) costs*. For instance, if you produce salsa, your list would include each and every raw material you use to make the salsa; the jar and lid that hold it; the label on the jar; the labor used to produce the salsa and the packaging; shipping costs you paid for any product component; the equipment or special tools used to produce the product; inventory control; and marketing. Yes, labor, shipping, equipment used, inventory control, and marketing are considered product components.

2) List the Cost of Each Product Component

Once you have your product component list for one jar of salsa, list the cost of each component.

Hard costs are easy to list, while more time and attention will be required to accurately identify soft costs such as labor. For example, you'd calculate the *labor component cost* based on the total dollar amount paid to people to produce the jars of salsa. So, to determine the labor cost associated with producing one jar of salsa, you take the total number of jars produced and divide them into the total dollar amount paid for the labor required to produce those jars. The result will be your labor component cost for one jar of salsa.

For equipment used to produce your product (another soft cost), divide the cost of the equipment by its expected lifespan. This will give you the depreciation value of the machine every minute or hour it is used for production. From there you can arrive at the *equipment component cost* for one individual product made by dividing the depreciation value by the number of units of those products.

Rule of Thumb: You arrive at individual hard and soft costs for one unit of product by taking the total hard and soft costs you paid for a full production run and dividing them by the number of products you produced.

3) Add the Costs of All Components to Arrive at Product Cost
Let's look at this example:

Sabrosa backpacks are the latest addition to the series of travel gear produced every year for the delight and comfort of those bitten by the travel bug. The backpacks are extremely stylish, of superior quality, and designed primarily for regular adventure travelers. They are strong enough to withstand all kinds of weather conditions and are enormously spacious and easy to carry. We will add up the cost of all components to arrive at the product cost of one backpack.

Hard Costs:
- Fabrics (polyester/nylon/PVC)—$56
- Chains—$15
- Straps—$18
- Zip puller—$8
- Packaging for each backpack—$28

Added up, these materials cost **$125**.

Soft Costs:
Determine your soft costs to produce one backpack. These costs include *labor charges*, *machine charges*, *marketing costs*, and *all other soft costs* associated with manufacturing the backpacks.

For this example, these additional costs add $37 to the hard costs.

Total Product Cost of One Backpack = Hard Costs ($125) + **Total Soft Costs** ($37) =$162

Calculate Your Product Cost:

_____

_____

_____

_____

_____

_____

_____

Step Twelve: Arrive at a Wholesale Price for Your Product

Now that you know your *product cost*, you can determine your product's *wholesale price*, the least expensive price you'd charge for your product that will still allow you to achieve a profit.

The following steps will help you arrive at this price:

1) Determine the General Market Price

Review market analysis and trend reports, target–market profiles, consumer surveys, and past performance reports on other companies with products similar to yours to determine the general market price.

2) Know and Understand Your Competition

Research your competition in target marketplaces to determine if your product meets, exceeds, or falls below their standards. Visit competitor websites and stores, and read reviews of competitor's products.

3) Set a Midrange Preliminary Wholesale Price for Your Product

A midrange wholesale price falls around the middle of the low to high prices set for products similar to yours that are already available in the marketplace. To create this price, use your product cost as a baseline and factor in all the manufacturing, marketing, consumer, and competition information you researched. This midrange price should, of course, be higher than your product cost to allow you to realize a profit. This preliminary price is not necessarily set in stone; if you plan to sell your product to a retailer, you can change this price, possibly shifting it up or down once you have established the type of *markups* or *margins* the retailer may impose on the product to arrive at their *sales price*. I'll go into a little more detail about this in the next step.

Determine Your Product's Wholesale Price:

_____

_____

_____

_____

_____

_____

_____

_____

_____

_____

Step Thirteen: Price Your Product for Maximum Profit

Now that you have a preliminary wholesale price, research what the retailers you'd like to sell to charge consumers for products that are similar to yours. If you find the wholesale price you've set is nearly identical to or very close to the actual sales price the store charges for similar products, you'll probably want to lower your wholesale price enough so that you are still meeting the profit goal you had set to make your product attractive to the retailer.

Remember, the sales price will be higher than the wholesale price so that the retailer can make a profit. The retailer will *mark up* your wholesale price to arrive at his or her *retail sales price*. Let's look at some definitions.

Markups and Margins

Markups and margins are different ways a retailer calculates his or her profit, and it's just as important for you to know how they arrive at these numbers as it is for them. Grasping this concept will put you on the path to pricing your product for maximum profit.

Markup is the retailer's profit expressed as a *percentage of the wholesale price*—what they paid you, the vendor.

Margin is the retailer's profit expressed as a *percentage of the retail sales price*.

Arriving at a Margin:
So, let's say a retailer buys a product from you for $5 and then sells it for $7.50. Your wholesale price to the retailer: $5 (Wholesale Price) + The retailer's profit on the sale: $2.50 (Profit Dollars) = The retailer's selling price on the shelf: $7.50 (Retail Price)

Margin = Profit as a Percentage of the Retail Price
So, calculate $2.50 of *profit* as a percentage of the *retail price* ($7.50) to get the *margin*.
So, $2.50 divided by $7.50 ($2.50/$7.50) = 33 percent.
So, this sales arrangement will give the retailer a 33 percent *margin*.

Arriving at a Markup:

Markup = Profit as a Percentage of the Wholesale Price
So, you'll calculate that $2.50 of *profit* as a percentage of *what they paid you* ($5), the vendor, to get the *markup*.
So, $2.50 divided by $5 ($2.50/$5) = 50 percent.
So this sales arrangement will give the retailer a 50 percent *markup*.

In both cases, you are still selling your product for $5, and the retailer is still making $2.50 on a $7.50 sale. The difference is simply which process the retailer uses to calculate that $7.50.

Margin and Markup Translation Matrix
Below is a matrix showing some of the most common margin/markup numbers and how to translate between them. Each of these pairs of numbers always translates to each other.

> 20% margin = 25% markup
> 25% margin = 33% markup
> 33% margin = 50% markup
> 37.5% margin = 60% markup
> 41% margin = 70% markup
> 44% margin = 80% markup
> 47% margin = 90% markup
> 50% margin = 100% markup

Markup to Margin and Margin to Markup

If you need to calculate a number not listed in the previous example, you can do it yourself easily.

When you know the markup, you can calculate the margin.

Margin = Markup Divided by (1 + markup)

Example – If you know the retailer uses a 70 percent markup:

$$
\begin{aligned}
\text{margin} &= .70 / (1 + 70\%) \\
&= .70 / (1 + .70) \\
&= .70 / 1.70 \\
&= 41\% \text{ margin}
\end{aligned}
$$

When you know the margin, you can calculate the markup.

Markup = Margin Divided by (1 – margin)

Example – If you know the retailer uses a 41 percent margin:

markup = .41 / (1 – .41)

.41 / .59

= approximately a 70% markup

Why Understanding Markup and Margin Is Important

Setting your wholesale price is one of the most important—and difficult—decisions you'll make as a product entrepreneur. Set your prices correctly and you'll have a better shot at making maximum profit by getting into retail stores when they buy your product in bulk.

Worksheets are provided at the back of this book to help you nail how to calculate sales markups and sales margins. You will also find a product cost worksheet model in the back. The lines below are provided for calculations related to your specific product.

Price Your Product for Maximum Profit:

_____

_____

_____

_____

_____

_____

_____

_____

_____

_____

_____

_____

Step Fourteen: Create a Product Brochure

Before all is said and done, create a product brochure to send out to potential stores, along with samples of your product, and have them on hand to give to potential customers and consumers at shows, fairs, and other events. Your package should:

- Position your company and product as a leader, enhance your reputation, and grow your client base
- Position you as the industry expert
- Build consumer confidence and trust
- Cultivate new markets
- Impress financial backers and encourage investors

Product Brochure Notes:

_____

_____

_____

_____

_____

_____

_____

_____

_____

Summing Up

As you can see, it takes many steps to bring your product to the marketplace. Don't get discouraged if the journey seems to be taking a little longer than you had hoped. Never forget that patience is a virtue and that this is especially true during the product development phase. Stay positive, roll with the punches, and keep your eyes on what your future product could become.

Think outside the bottle.

Next up, we'll look at how to choose the right manufacturer (for you).

THINKING OUTSIDE THE BOTTLE

_____

_____

_____

_____

_____

_____

_____

_____

_____

_____

Me cooking up a batch of my bell pepper salsa at the
Ashburn Sauce Company, Virginia Beach, Virginia

The original Sabrosa jar everyone said
looked like a jar of hair grease

My daughter, Ashley, sporting the Sabrosa brand

The evolution of the Asorbas label and brand

Me and Rodney Eason, my first investor. Thanks, Rodney!

Me at my first farmers' market

Sabrosa on a Farm Fresh store shelf
beside a Paula Deen food product

Working a trade show

My medium bell pepper salsa wins Best New Product
at the Virginia Food & Beverage Expo

My salsa wins Director's Choice Award
at the State Fair of Virginia

Sabrosa enters 60 Farm Fresh stores and other outlets

My mentor Michele Hoskins,
CEO of Michele Foods

My grandmother Alma Echoles—It all started
with this lady and a garden

#79 DUANE THOMPSON
DT 6-1 235 FR
Hampton, VA Hampton H.S.

College Days, Virginia State University

My mom, Patricia Thompson, was always my biggest fan.

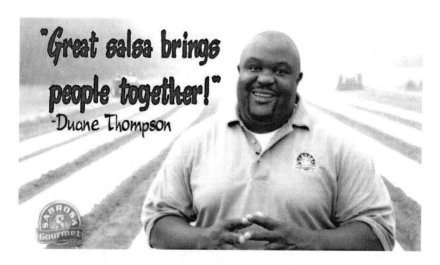

"Great salsa brings people together!"
-Duane Thompson

A picture on my website, www.asorbas.com

Asorbas being manufactured at
the Ashburn Sauce Company plant

Inside Business
The Hampton Roads Business Journal

Duane Thompson, 39 Managing
Director, Sabrosa Foods Inc.

"...I have always kept the little chopper to remind me of how far I've come and never forget the modest beginnings of Sabrosa Foods Inc."

One of my many local print articles

CHAPTER 6

WHEN YOU FIND THE RIGHT MANUFACTURER, SAY "I DO"

"The relationship you have with your
manufacturer is like a marriage."
—Duane Thompson

YOU MAY HAVE your business plan and product development down to a science, but if you aren't working with the right manufacturer you could lose the selling game before you even begin to compete. Before you begin your manufacturer search, keep two things top of mind:

First, choose a manufacturer that's close to your home and business. Here's why: You can frequently check on whether your product is being manufactured according to your agreement and expectations, and driving a few miles is cheaper and quicker than flying or taking a train. Also, if your product happens to primarily be sold locally or in your home state, as was the case for Asorbas for many years, and your manufacturer also assists with distributing your product, you'll cut down on the costs of getting your product to stores.

Second, work with a *turnkey* manufacturer that will produce and package your product and assist you with its distribution. This will allow you to focus on sales. Not being able to do so could mean the difference between remaining in business or not. So you see, the manufacturer you work with could determine your business outcome. So now, let's help you find the right one.

Tips for Finding the Right Manufacturer

Check Out the Manufacturer's Reputation

Before you pick up the phone or shoot an e–mail to start your conversation with a manufacturer, check out their reputation. Google them, ask people with products similar to yours to tell you who is who in the manufacturing business and what others say about them. Don't write a manufacturer off because of one person's experience or even a couple of people's experiences. Try to get a healthy amount of opinions, then draw your conclusions.

The Manufacturer Should Ask You to Sign a Confidentiality Agreement

Let's say you now have a list of manufacturers you're interested in. First, in your initial talks with a potential manufacturer, he or she should request that you sign a confidentiality agreement before either of you exchanges critical information. If they don't do this, it speaks volumes about whether you should proceed. It's standard practice to have that agreement in place, and if the manufacturer refuses the reasons could range from them being new to business themselves or to something nefarious. Once, a manufacturing company I was considering did not offer a confidentiality agreement. Later, I discovered the company had been sued several times. One of the claims was that the company was making and selling an entrepreneur's product without disclosing the sales and was pocketing the money.

The Manufacturer Should Understand Your Product's Regulations

You should verify whether the manufacturer understands your product's regulations. The onus is on you to know what laws surround your product *before* you meet with the manufacturer; you need to know what you're *not* being told. For example, any third–party manufacturer of food goods should know that a *batch code* (a code that shows when the product was produced) must be applied to your product and submitted to the Food and Drug Administration (FDA) for recall purposes. If they don't, don't do business with them.

The Manufacturer Should Have Liability Insurance

Find out whether the manufacturer has product liability insurance and if they'll be willing to indemnify you (to compensate you for losses or damage) or add your product to their policy as additionally insured. If the manufacturer says no to any of these questions, stop interviewing them and start looking elsewhere. With liability insurance, if the product is recalled or defective, the manufacturer—not you—is liable for covering the costs associated with the recall or defect and their insurance should help them cover it. But don't just take their word that they have the insurance. If they don't offer to show you their certificate of insurance, ask to see it at your initial meeting. Don't stop there. After you've left the meeting, call the insurance company or broker to verify that the certificate and the company's coverage are valid.

The Manufacturer Should Let You Speak with Its Top Employees and Clients

The person you're interviewing should let you interview other top company employees. If they give you a hard time over this, this could be a red flag signaling you should walk away from the talks. The manufacturer should also provide names of other companies they've worked with. When you speak with these contacts, you'll want to ask them to describe their relationship with the manufacturer: Did the company meet deadlines? Was the product produced up to or above standards? What problems, if any, were encountered? Overall, did the manufacturer do a good job, and if so, how?

The Manufacturer Should Give You Samples

The manufacturer should be willing to give you samples of raw materials they would use to make your product. For instance, if your product is salsa, you want to ensure that the manufacturer does not use rotten tomatoes.

The Manufacturer Should Let You Tour Their Facility

You should also ask to see the manufacturer's product–producing equipment. This means you should be touring the manufacturing facility. Note whether the manufacturer allows you to walk the floors with ease or restricts your tour. If it's the latter, ask why access is limited. There could be a perfectly good explanation. For example, a product run could be happening, making it dangerous to be on the manufacturing floor. The reason for a limited tour could also be to conceal something. Be skeptical. Maybe the manufacturer wants to hide something that would dissuade you from signing a contract.

During the tour you'll want to examine the machinery. Is it clean and in good working condition? You'll want to look at the floor. Do you see food droppings, rodent droppings? Remember, you're looking for an environment conducive to manufacturing your product. Use all five senses when you're assessing the facility; rely on your sixth sense too. What overall vibe do you get? Does the place feel like a good fit for you and your product?

The Manufacturer Should Assist with Shipping Your Product to Stores or Other Outlets

You also need to find out whether the manufacturer will ship your finished product to stores or other outlets. If they don't, and you decide to work with them, you're on the hook for getting your product to the marketplace or finding a distribution company to do it for you. An experienced manufacturer will work with a transporter that can ship your goods. Some small manufacturers just getting into the business don't do this. You really have to ask yourself whether you want to work with a startup or fairly new manufacturer or if it's in your product's and company's best interest to work with an established outlet. Some things to consider: In addition to not offering to transport your product, a newbie manufacturer may not have adequate space to house your product. Remember, you want to grow along with the manufacturer; you don't want the manufacturer to grow along with you.

Additionally, I urge you to work with a manufacturer that can assist you with shipping your product because I know firsthand what can happen when you distribute your product yourself. Though Mama Vida distributed my product during my business's early days, after a few years with them I took on some distribution duties myself to cut costs. I did in fact save a few dollars, but ultimately I found running around to stores was a terrible use of my time—I was working "in the business and not on the business." Avoid this!

Find Out Where the Manufacturer's Products Are Sold and Check Them Out

If you know a certain product can be found at Target, for example, visit the store to check it out. Does it look professionally made? If you have enough money to cover it, buy the product and try it out at home. Does it live up to its claims? If it's a food product, does it taste good, fresh? If it's a toy, is it well put together and do all the parts work? While in the store, talk with the workers who put the product on the shelves. What can they tell you about how it sells? Does it sit on the shelf for long? Is it in demand? What do consumers say about it? You can ask the clerk at the checkout counter the same questions. They may be able to provide anecdotal information about the product's sales.

Marrying Your Manufacturer

You may not stay with your first manufacturer forever. A few years after I relocated from Maryland back to Virginia, I switched from doing business with Maryland–based Mama Vida to Ashburn Sauce Company, just a city over from what is now Sabrosa's Norfolk, Virginia, headquarters (I left Hampton some years ago). Your first manufacturer, like your first boyfriend or girlfriend, is important. They can set the tone for your product's success, or lack thereof, for years to come.

As for my now long–standing relationship with Ashburn, it's like a marriage. I don't see myself leaving Hampton Roads any time soon, and I'll probably be with Ashburn for quite some time.

Take your marriage to your manufacturer seriously. Find the right one for your product and walk into the sunset of product success.

In our next chapter, we'll look at why it pays to initially sell your product locally.

**

Use "Thinking Outside the Bottle" to answer the following questions:

1. What's the manufacturer's reputation?
2. Does the manufacturer ask you to sign a confidentiality agreement?
3. Does the manufacturer understand your product's regulations?
4. Does the manufacturer have liability insurance?
5. Will the manufacturer let you talk with other top employees of his/her company and put you in touch with other companies they work with? What information did the employees and companies share with you?
6. Will the manufacturer give you samples of product they produce? How do those samples appear?
7. Will the manufacturer let you tour the facility? What did you see on the tour? What impressed you? What concerned you?
8. Will the manufacturer ship your product to stores or other outlets? How far away will the manufacturer ship? How much does the shipping service add on to your contract price?
9. What contract price is the manufacturer offering you? How does this price stack up to other manufacturers' prices?
10. Where are the manufacturer's products sold? If you've taken a trip to the store to check out the products, how do they appear? Do they look professionally produced, adhere to regulations, etc.?

THINKING OUTSIDE THE BOTTLE

_____

_____

_____

_____

_____

_____

_____

_____

_____

_____

_____

_____

_____

_____

_____

_____

_____

_____

_____

_____

_____

_____

_____

_____

_____

_____

_____

_____

_____

_____

_____

_____

_____

_____

_____

CHAPTER 7

SELLING YOUR PRODUCT— WHY IT PAYS TO START LOCALLY

"A local approach allows the entrepreneur to be more customer/client/media accessible, to better understand costs associated with product development, and to begin to build brand recognition."
—Duane Thompson

NOW THAT YOU'VE successfully developed your product, it's time to start selling it!

Where do you begin? In your backyard.

I don't mean this literally—but almost. Unless you have sufficient financial resources to sustain a campaign to market and advertise your product and to pay support staff, I strongly recommend you start out selling it locally, in your hometown and no farther than the boundaries of your state.

There are numerous benefits of doing this, at least initially. For instance, if you're a first–time self–published author, and therefore an unknown commodity in the world of literature, who is more likely to buy your book at your bookstore signing? Friends, family, coworkers, and locals who may like the idea of supporting one of their own. Who is more likely to provide press coverage? The local newspaper, radio station, and online publication or blogger.

Starting out locally allows you to deeply penetrate a market segment and, by focusing on one area, to thoroughly understand how to meet consumer needs and demand. When you stay local, you can also guerilla market like crazy! Practically speaking, you may also spend less on travel. And saving money on transportation costs means you'll have more money to invest in your product.

Before I branched into markets outside Virginia, I sold a lot of salsa at events within a fifty–mile radius of my Hampton Roads, Virginia, home. Suddenly I became the "local guy" selling a hot new salsa, and this alone had value.

In short, starting out at home PAYS. You're concentrating your marketing efforts in a smaller sphere, which can have several other important benefits:

- You may make fewer units of the product, which can keep your production costs at a reasonable level.
- You increase the chances of selling the product—people like to buy local, as noted in the newbie author example.
- You increase the chances of the product becoming a household name.
- You will be more accessible to consumers.
- You increase the chances of receiving free media coverage.

All these factors can lead to a higher demand for the product, and this demand will help you set your product's price.

Besides the obvious places to sell—stores and in my case, farmers' markets—staying local provides other less obvious marketing opportunities. Here are a few to consider:

- Your Relationships—Don't dismiss your local professional and personal relationships. Your contacts may offer to let you sell or promote your product at a business event or at a home party or the like.
- Your Community—Sell your product at local events. For instance, pay to set up a booth at annual community festivals, and keep an eye out on the dates when the local churches and

civic groups hold their flea markets. Check whether your bank rents rooms for sales or other marketing events. You may be surprised.

- Local Charity Groups—Get involved with philanthropic organizations. Sabrosa Foods donates salsa to a foodbank fundraiser every year. There, we meet food store representatives whose businesses have also donated to the fundraiser. These are businesses Sabrosa might do business with in the future.

- Local or Regional Trade Shows—You can see what your local competition charges for a similar product and how your product's sales stack up against theirs. The shows also allow you to see how your competitors pitch their products and to listen to consumer feedback about what they're selling.

A Quick Word about Selling Online

Selling locally doesn't mean you shouldn't sell online. When you set up your business website, you should provide a purchase link for viewers all over the US—and even overseas, if you're willing to work with customs rules—if you think you can manage online sales to national and international consumers. You'll need a way to cost–effectively and time–effectively ship them the goods and still realize a profit. Remember, your job is to focus on sales, not to get bogged down in distribution.

Selling online, however, will, for a number of reasons, not be quite the same as "live" sales.

While your manufacturer may help transport your product to stores, they may not send out individual products for one–off orders. There are a few things you can do to be in a position to fulfill these orders, though:

- Wherever you do business (home, a rented space, etc.), keep a supply of your product on hand to send out for online orders, and then ship the product to the consumer yourself.

- If you anticipate the demand for online orders will be bigger than your home or office space, and you don't have time to monitor sales and ship your goods, you can work with a fulfillment house, a business that will store, manage, and ship your product.

I can vouch for the effectiveness of working with a fulfillment house. While you will pay to use the service, you may be able to make more money because this business is devoted to helping you with your online sales. For example, a fulfillment house I worked with shipped far, far more jars of my salsa than I had the capacity to handle. Furthermore, by working with the company, my product margins were higher, which means I made more money on the online salsa orders than I would have made on my own.

- If you don't have the financial resources to work with a fulfillment house and the time or capacity to monitor online sales, you could enlist a trustworthy, businesswise family member or close friend and pay them a fee that works for you and for them.

Keep in mind that whether you're personally shipping your product or working with a fulfillment house, family member, or friend, your product's online price should be higher than its physical–store shelf price. Why? You need to compensate for the costs associated with establishing and maintaining a sales website and the services you buy to boost traffic to the site. Also, the shipping price should cover all costs associated with mailing the product—the box, tape, label, stuffing, and gas. Asorbas's online price is slightly higher than the store price, yet each year its online sales grow. Have I received complaints about the online price? Yes. But there are also people who complain about the price in stores. You will never please everybody.

The Beauty of Starting Out Locally for Asorbas

While I advise you to set up an online commerce tool on your website if it makes business sense for you, personally, I did not sell Asorbas online right away, and that worked for me.

Starting out locally with live sales has been a key to Asorbas's rise. My salsa can now be found well outside Virginia, but it wouldn't have traveled that far if I hadn't started building my brand right in my backyard. The buzz about heartburn and reflux–free salsa started at the local swap meets, arts and craft and state fairs, farmers' markets, Farm Fresh food stores, and other local venues. As I got the salsa in front of more people, awareness of my product rose and so did my sales. These results provided a better picture of how to run these markets. As time wore on, I began predicting, with an error margin of 15 percent either way, just how much salsa I would sell. I got a better sense of how much product I needed to take to the events. Starting out locally allowed me to key into my target market, and to discover, from trial and error, how to land sales.

The local strategy created a demand for the salsa and a buzz. That buzz germinated over several years locally and grew like a healthy crop, moving beyond its original area of planting and into other zones. By word of mouth, consumers were spreading the good news about Asorbas, and its reputation helped the salsa receive lots of free and positive local media coverage. (You can check out much of the publicity on Sabrosa's YouTube page, https://www.youtube.com/user/Datassoc1.)

In most cases, you'll have to go after the local coverage, which I'll cover in–depth in the next chapter. But strong local sales of a strong local product increase your chances of getting it.

Positive press coverage can help you take your product to the next level. That coverage lives forever online, and it can allow you to show the rest of the world—outside of your local one—that your product has a good reputation and sells well. That, in turn, can give you a better shot at branching out of your local market and selling your product in other areas.

That's what most of us want.

That's what happened for Asorbas.

**

In "Thinking Outside the Bottle," brainstorm potential local venues where your product could be sold and how you could tap into your relationships, community, charity groups, and local or regional trade shows and other events to promote it.

THINKING OUTSIDE THE BOTTLE

_____

_____

_____

_____

_____

_____

_____

_____

_____

_____

_____

_____

_____

_____

_____

_____

_____

_____

_____

_____

_____

_____

_____

CHAPTER 8

DON'T PAY FOR ADVERTISING WHEN THE MEDIA WILL DO IT FOR FREE

"If you're doing it right, the media will come."
—Duane Thompson

UNTIL 2015, I'D never paid for advertising. NEVER. That year, I launched my first TV commercial (https://youtube/HqTgfEDdLjk). It was part of my strategy to expand Asorbas's geographic reach. Yet even when I wasn't paying for advertising, Sabrosa Foods received a lot of publicity, first locally and then nationally, on TV, radio, in print, and online. There is a method to landing media coverage, and you're about to learn it. This method can help you increase your bottom line while preventing unnecessary advertising bills.

Again, it all goes back to starting locally. First, as mentioned in the previous chapter, you've already overcome a hurdle to local media coverage by starting out at home. But now that you have this ace in the hole, to ensure you'll actually get the coverage you must have a solid product and have built positive word of mouth through local sales. After this, you'll have to learn how to communicate this great news about your product to your local media.

So how do you get the word out to TV stations, newspapers, and websites?

First, create a media package. This is a printed or electronic binder of material that should include:

- What your product is and what makes it unique
- Boilerplate product information—price, unique number identifier, where product is sold
- Who you are. Briefly tell your story—the reason you're selling the product
- Your business and e–mail addresses, phone and fax numbers— also include a business card
- Consumer accolades, industry awards
- Media coverage—provide links to online videos and full copies of newspaper and magazine articles and other print coverage

Media Kit Specifications

Your media kit should be professionally produced and not overwhelming. I won't specify a number of pages, but I advise that the kit be lean enough so that a reporter or editor could skim it in five minutes or less and know exactly why they should put you in the spotlight. Additionally, the typeface on the kit's interior pages should be black, clean, and easy to read (Times New Roman is an example). If you're not a wordsmith, hire a writer and editor to ensure the kit effectively communicates its message and is free of typos.

Include a cover letter addressed to the specific media recipient. You can use a form letter that you alter slightly to fit the particular target you're trying to hit. Next, your cover page should feature your product name, logo, slogan (my page said the "No Acid Reflux" "No Heartburn Salsa"), website address, and a clear picture of your product.

As noted in the bulleted list in this chapter, you should also have a product information page. This page will, of course, show your product's name and logo, but it should also address what your product does, what it solves, and why it's better than its competitors. Additionally, this page should also include your business, e–mail, and website addresses, as well as phone and fax numbers.

Here's what my kit's product information page says:

Asorbas all–natural roasted bell pepper salsa is the essential condiment for heartburn and acid reflux sufferers because of its simple no–preservatives acidic neutralizing formula and the cooking process used to make it. Asorbas features a vitamin C–rich roasted bell pepper base seasoned with all–natural herbs and vegetables picked at the peak of freshness. They are blended with an aged balsamic vinegar, which renders a unique flavor excellent for cooking, dipping, grilling, or marinating.

What does it do?
- *Naturally neutralizes acid to help ease digestion.*
- *The healthy flavor–enhanced formulation may be added in place of ketchup, relishes, or chutneys; blended into ground turkey or beef; used as a dip for gatherings and dinner parties; used in soup bases as an MSG alternative; added to current low–calorie diet programs.*
- *Provides vitamin C and antioxidant (lycopene).*
- *Adds nutrition from fresh vegetables and 3 natural herbs.*
- *PH–balanced shelf stable formula up to 2 years.*
- *Does not contain preservatives and is gluten free.*

Who needs it?
- *Asorbas is a "must have" healthy food condiment formulated for flavor and easy digestion.*
- *It is also intended to be used as an alternative to other condiments containing unnatural preservatives.*
- *Any consumer looking to infuse flavor through cooking, marinating, or dipping without harsh digestion will need and appreciate the simplicity, power, and effectiveness of Sabrosa's all–natural roasted bell pepper salsa.*

Why Asorbas instead of other salsas?
- *Asorbas's simple all–natural ingredients, fire–roasting formulation, and balsamic vinegar infusion process provides*

> *uncompromised health attributes and flavor enhancements unmatched by any other market brand available today.*
> - *Even after other salsa manufacturers release their interpretation of healthy all–natural products, Asorbas will remain the clear choice because of its commitment to providing healthy all–natural foods through flavorful alternative gourmet condiments.*

In addition to printed information, your media kit should also include a sample of your product. I always send at least one full-size jar of Asorbas with mine.

Now that you have the basis for your kit, here's how you go about sending it:

- Do Your Research: Scour the local newspapers, TV stations, and websites to find out who covers the topic (or topics) related to your product. Document their e–mail and physical work addresses and phone numbers. In my case, I identified every reporter, editor, and freelancer who covered anything connected to food.
- Adjust your form letter accordingly, and send it, along with your media kit and product, to the appropriate media person.
- Follow up with the media contact within three days of sending the kit.

Question: So what if you don't hear back from the contact? Even after you've e–mailed them a follow–up note or left a voicemail?

Answer: You don't give up.

When my packages didn't elicit a response, a month or so later I sent the contact another package with another jar of salsa and an updated note letting them know what had since happened (any new awards the salsa had received or new stores it was being sold in). If you're serious about selling, you have to be persistent. Don't think you're bugging the reporter or editor—it's their job to field story pitches.

Because of my persistence, one newspaper article led to another. I also appeared on a local morning program where I was featured mixing my salsa, and I was covered in a local magazine—after repeatedly sending the magazine media kits, it featured Asorbas, then still called "Sabrosa," in a full–page spread. As you start amassing media coverage, include it in your kit. Remember, the media *loves* to jump on the bandwagon. If everyone else is covering you then you *must* be a hot commodity, and a hot commodity is news. News coverage will beget more news coverage.

In the Asorbas media kits, I promoted the salsa as if it were the best thing since the beginning of time. I revealed how I stumbled upon making it, touted its health benefits, its awards (the Best New Food Product Winner at the 2008 Virginia Food & Beverage Expo, the 2009 Virginia State Fair's Director's Choice Award, and the local journal Inside Business's 2010 Entrepreneur of the Year award), and what consumers said about its great taste. I focused on how the salsa is a staple product everyone should have in their refrigerator.

After a media outlet covered the salsa, I kept in touch with them. I'd send the editor or reporter updated information when something new or big happened. The media is always looking for stories, and "a local person makes good" angle never loses its appeal.

The newspeople made me and Asorbas look so good, readers probably thought I was making a million dollars. Truth is, even with all that coverage, I wasn't making much of anything in those early years; but the coverage broadened Asorbas's profile and built a bigger demand for the product—which eventually helped it become a moneymaker.

In a sense, the media legitimized the product. In many people's minds, if the press covers you, you are "important." Eventually, far more organizations sought me out to participate in their events; the local Small Business Administration office, for example, interviewed me for inclusion in an annual report, and Sabrosa's home base, the city of Norfolk, requested my company produce a salsa and promote it as Norfolk "made." Of course, I jumped on that.

I was guerilla marketing all over the place, and with the success in Farm Fresh and the abundance of local media coverage, I knew it was time to knock on the national media's door. So I sent my press kits, filled with all my local press coverage, to big media outlets across the country—and they bit!

Asorbas and I were featured on MSNBC and Phil Lempert–Supermarket Guru, who rated our salsa a nine out of ten—and we did about an additional $7,000 in sales immediately after Lempert's segment aired the first time. Then one day, I found a letter in my mailbox from Mark Burnett, the producer of the reality–TV show *Survivor*. He wanted me to come out to Hollywood to appear on a new show called *Shark Tank*. Rodney Eason and I were flown out to Studio City, where we shot some of the show. Ultimately, we mostly wound up on the cutting room floor, but for the rest of my life—and the life of Asorbas—I will always be able to claim in my press kits that I was one of the first contestants on *Shark Tank*.

Other Free Opportunities: The Internet and Social Media

As a budding entrepreneur, the Internet should be one of the top tools on your marketing list. The first thing I advise you to do is create a website for your company and product. If you're tech savvy and think you can build a site on your own, give it a try; but I advise most of you to leave the website building to a professional.

This doesn't mean you shouldn't be involved in the website's creation. Far from it. You should be bringing ideas to the table. Let the designer know what you want your website to achieve (to sell you and your product to your target audience), and be specific about what information it needs to cover. Because you're still getting a business off the ground, I advise that you not complicate your website with features like a blog. Creating a blog creates work. You or someone else—someone who you would presumably pay—has to fill that beast at least a few times a month. At this point, the blog is not worth it.

Here are the main features your product website should cover initially:

- Homepage (Shows your product, logo, name, what it is, and what problem it solves)

Tabs on the homepage should include:

- Product Details (Provides more information about the product, including its price)
- About Us (Your story—who you are and why you created the product)
- Click to Buy (A link that allows the viewer to buy the product online—put this link up if you have the capacity to handle online orders)
- Locations (Stores where consumers can find the product)
- Consumer Recommendations and Product Commendations

You may choose to hire a college student to provide good, inexpensive help to design and maintain your website, or you may hire a professional designer. Prices for website creation and maintenance are wide ranging. I've heard them vary from as low as a couple of hundred dollars to at least $2,500. You'll want to do your research before you decide.

Other Internet Tools

At minimum, you should establish Facebook and Twitter pages for your product and link them to your website. These two media tools will allow you to build your audience and promote your product for free. With the click of a button you can update followers on sales, promotions, and other events. These sites help you build brand recognition. Sabrosa Foods created a presence on social media several years ago. Now, a lot of people who would have otherwise not heard of us know our name and have become loyal consumers.

A Last Word on Media Coverage: The Key to Receiving More of It

Just because you've received a lot of media coverage doesn't mean you should stop pursuing it. Always look for opportunities to get your business back in the positive media spotlight.

Anytime something significant happens—for example, if you win a major grant, a major contract, introduce a new product, or expand the stores your product is being sold in—call up the media and propose a story.

One of Sabrosa Foods's significant happenings, of course, is the renaming of our salsa.

The media pitch goes something like this:

Why the name change? Our salsa stands out from the crowd, and it was time for its name to stand out too. So I invented the name Asorbas. It didn't exist before I thought it up. Now it's copyrighted, and NO ONE else can have it or will EVER HAVE it. With the new name, sales are up locally and everywhere else our salsa is now sold.

**

Use "Thinking Outside the Bottle" to plan a media kit, your media list, media pitch (what you'll say in one paragraph to hook the media on your story), and your estimated schedule for sending out media kits.

In the next chapter, we'll look at model product entrepreneurs. They are great examples of how to successfully launch a product.

THINKING OUTSIDE THE BOTTLE

_____

_____

_____

_____

_____

_____

_____

_____

_____

_____

_____

_____

_____

_____

_____

_____

_____

_____

_____

_____

_____

_____

_____

_____

_____

_____

_____

_____

_____

_____

_____

_____

_____

_____

_____

_____

CHAPTER 9

A PERFECT TEN: CASE STUDIES

*"As an entrepreneur, you're the one who is going
to be the life or death of your business."*
—Duane Thompson

AS YOU'VE SEEN so far in *Think Outside the Bottle*, launching a product into the marketplace takes a lot of perseverance and passion; but to give it a real shot at succeeding, there are ten attributes it must have. In this chapter, you'll meet two passionate, persevering entrepreneurs whose products have these attributes. These businesspeople and their products are what I call *Perfect Tens*.

The Ten Perfect Product Qualities

1. Product meets a genuine consumer need
2. Product has strong price–value relationship
3. Product has effective distribution channels
4. Product can scale up (produce more product to meet demand)
5. Product has sufficient funding
6. Product has organizational support
7. Product makes financial sense
8. Product is part of an overall brand–building campaign
9. Product has a great marketing plan
10. Product is in the right place at the right time

Case Study One
Entrepreneur: Carolyn A. Brent
Product: Book

Many years ago, Carolyn A. Brent says she fought some of her siblings in court for the right to continue being their elderly father's primary caregiver, a role she says she had filled for twelve years. The court case wore her out, and she says she lost the stamina to keep fighting it. When she finally put her situation into perspective, she realized she wanted to change some elder care–related laws so that no one else would endure what she had—losing the right to care for an elderly parent.

Brent's quest led her to libraries, where she attempted to research how to effectively work with siblings to care for a parent. She says she couldn't find anything on the topic, so she decided to create a book to address it. But before Brent began writing, she wanted to make sure she wouldn't be reinventing the wheel. She hired a marketer to help her further look for any books covering the topic of sibling disagreements that erupt during end–of–life care for an ailing parent. When she was satisfied there was nothing substantial in the marketplace, she wrote *Why Wait? The Baby Boomers' Guide to Preparing Emotionally, Financially and Legally for a Parent's Death.*

With a completed book in hand, Brent had met *Perfect Ten* attribute one: Her product met a genuine consumer need. It addressed a problem many adult children struggle with, providing information to help them navigate an oftentimes difficult situation.

From here on, we will examine how Brent met the other Perfect Ten attributes.

- Brent's book had a strong **price–value relationship**: For less than $20, Brent says, readers received advice from an elder law attorney who is certified in California and vetted throughout the country. Her book is also filled with advice from healthcare professionals, psychologists, psychiatrists, certified hospice care workers (MDs, RNs, and MDs) on the topic of elder caregiving, as well as Brent's own harrowing tale and learned lessons on the topic.

- Brent's book traveled through **effective distribution channels**: She made it available in all of the major online bookstores, including Amazon and Barnes & Noble, and for ordering directly from bookstores.

- *Why Wait?* could **scale up** when required: Brent self-published her book, so she made it a print–on–demand title. That means *Why Wait?* was printed only when a consumer paid for it—so there would always be a book available no matter the demand.

- The book had **sufficient funding**: Brent used personal savings to finance the endeavor. She'd been a high-grossing pharmaceutical sales rep and had the resources to bankroll a $79,000 investment in her project.

- She had **organizational support**: Brent says her project was supported by the American Association of Retired People (AARP) and the board of directors of a local Alzheimer's support group. "The vice president of the elder law division of the AARP was in support," says Brent. "He verified that this was a national issue, vetted my book free of charge, and endorsed it." She says an elder law attorney also vetted the book for no fee.

- The product launch made **financial sense**: Brent made a big investment in *Why Wait?* that paid off. While she has not financially recovered what she put into the book, the payoff came when Harlequin, a major publishing house, came knocking with a contract to pay her to publish her second book on the same topic. This gets back to the idea that you start off with one product and have to earn the right to produce a second product, which Brent certainly did.

- *Why Wait?* was part of an overall **brand–building campaign**: Brent used the book to further promote her profile as an "elder–care legislation" advocate. The book is heavily featured on her professional website, and she sells or promotes it at public engagements, where she speaks on the topic of elder–care legislation.

- Brent had a **great marketing plan**: She paid a marketing firm nearly $30,000 to ensure she was featured by major national TV, radio, print, and online media—*CNN Reports* and the *Washington Times* among them. She says she was also featured on local NBC, ABC, and CBS–TV affiliates in San Francisco, San Jose, and Sacramento, California, as well as in Seattle, Washington, and Washington, DC. She also used social media and a website to promote her product.

- Brent's book hit **in the right place at the right time**: Baby boomers' parents are now old enough to require caregiving, and her book was published when many boomers could use a self–help book on the caregiving topic—and it went on to become a number one Amazon bestseller.

In her own words, Brent describes how she went from success with *Why Wait?* to the Harlequin contract for *The Caregiver's Companion*, an expansion of her first book:

> *I was very passionate about the subject matter. I never did it with the intent that I'd be rich one day. I went in with the mindset of I'm going to put money behind this because I want to change laws. So my passion forced me to dig deeper into my pocket, and because of my passion, now the commission is starting to come in. With the national publication of* The Caregiver's Companion, *people are constantly asking me to be on their shows. And now I host a TV segment of my own, "Across the Ages," on an NTV ABC show called* The

Good Life, *and I've become a spokesperson for the American Association of Retired People. Everything that's happening now stems from* Why Wait? *And while I paid all the expenses to publish* Why Wait?, *Harlequin is paying for* The Caregiver's Companion. *With a major publisher behind me, now I'm able to command high public–speaking fees. Harlequin has taken me where I could have never taken myself. My book is now literally sold in the US and abroad.*

A Big Takeaway from Brent's Story

It's not featured on the Perfect Ten list because the list focuses on product qualities, but one of the biggest takeaways from Brent's product journey is her story—a compelling, personal reason inspired her to write *Why Wait?* As I said earlier in *Think Outside the Bottle*, people buy you before they buy your product. Supporters bought Brent, then they bought into her book. Then Brent sealed her sales success by ensuring her product met all the criteria on the Perfect Ten Product list—and the result is a "perfect" business outcome.

Case Study Two
Entrepreneur: Leslie Crews
Product: Tea

Leslie Crews and her tea, Kombuchick (a twist on the name "kombucha," the effervescent black or green tea with Asian origins), are making strides in the marketplace. I know this personally.

For several years, I've mentored Crews as she's worked on bringing her product to life and to stores. Because it's fermented, it has a short shelf life, so I've been helping her find a formulation to keep the brew fresher longer. I've also helped her meet necessary regulations so she can legally sell it.

But more than that, I've helped Crews hone her personal story so that when she tries to connect with consumers or land media coverage, she has a fighting chance at selling her tea or being put in the media spotlight.

The results have been stellar. In recent years, Crews has won awards for her work and for Kombuchick, including the Service Corps of Retired Executives Foundation's 2013 Outstanding Young Entrepreneur Award. She's also been covered by local and national media.

In the short time Crews has sold Kombuchick, she's already exhibited the Perfect Ten traits for product sales success. But as she's still working on product one, and has far fewer financial resources than Case Study One's Brent, her story offers some different insights on what it takes to be a Perfect Ten.

Let's examine them:

- The product meets a **genuine consumer need**: Kombucha tea has been around for centuries and long been popular with the alternative–health crowd. Advertised as promoting a healthy digestive system and immune function, it is fermented by adding a culture of bacteria and yeast to a solution of tea, sugar, and sometimes fruit juice and other flavorings. Consumers' rising awareness about the benefits of this drink and the fact it's popping up in health food markets all over the United States shows Crews's version of it, Kombuchick, will push a genuine consumer hot button.

- Kombuchick has a **strong price–value relationship**: Kombuchick's price–to–value business model seemed perfectly matched and well suited for Crews's targeted demographic. The model is based on the premise that health–conscious consumers will pay a bit more when products are claiming health benefits. It's OK to claim the health benefits as long as they are true—as I mentioned in Chapter 5, federal regulations are very specific about not making false claims. Kombuchick's model was similar to Asorbas's earlier model—the "no acid reflux," "no heartburn" message.

- Kombuchick has **effective distribution channels**: Kombuchick has not partnered with an outside distribution firm. Crews is still in the early stages of building her business and handles logistics in–house—she personally drives her tea to stores and stocks it on shelves. As I mentioned earlier, typically I don't advise this distribution method, but at this point in the development of Crews's business it's working for her because her tea is turning a profit.

- Kombuchick is able to **scale up when required**: Crews's business model allows for scale up without compromising product performance or losing revenue. She has accomplished this by successfully identifying and testing Kombuchick's core market. The company has also aligned itself with financial and business resources to allow for scaling. Crews has positioned her company to anticipate scale up by understanding her product production processes and methods so that she can fully automate them in the near future, which will free her up to boost product marketing and outsource nonessential sales work, such as graphic design and human resources.

- It has **sufficient funding**: Crews's product pricing is set to ensure that with each sale the tea not only pays for itself but makes a hefty return. She has identified financial milestones to indicate when the time will be right to move the company into the next stage of scalability. By growing the company in this way, she ensures Kombuchick is always sufficiently funded, minimizes unnecessary debt, and financially stabilizes the firm while in the startup stage.

- It has **organizational support**: Crews has secured organizational support by building a trust network of professionals who she places in strategic positions best suited to provide advice respective to their areas of expertise.

- The product launch **made financial sense**: Crews took money from her savings account and also relied on cash gifts from Kombuchick's fans to assist with its production in its earliest days, so she had the resources and support to make the launch happen.

- It's part of an overall **brand–building campaign**: Crews has identified her product brand–building campaign. It is based off of building a social awareness movement with the slogan "Join the Bevolotion." She stresses the product brand and company philosophy in all media and interviews she does.

- It has a **great marketing plan**: Crews's marketing plan allows for local exposure and is designed to grow as sales increase. Using marketing tips I've shared with her, she's been covered by the local media and also landed a one–page feature in a national magazine, *Entrepreneur*. Grabbing national coverage so early in the game, the sky is the limit for Kombuchick.

Summing Up

Is your product a Perfect Ten or is it on its way to getting there? If it's not, what will it take to meet the ten criteria that Brent and Crews have mastered? Use "Thinking Outside the Bottle" to write down which criteria your product meets—and how—and what you can do to help it meet the criteria if it doesn't.

In the next chapter, we'll look at top factors that cause product entrepreneurs to fail—and what you can do to avoid this fate. You'll find that the reasons a product fails don't always have to do with the merits of the product itself.

THINKING OUTSIDE THE BOTTLE

_____

_____

_____

_____

_____

_____

_____

_____

_____

_____

_____

_____

_____

_____

_____

_____

_____

_____

_____

_____

_____

_____

_____

_____

_____

_____

_____

_____

_____

_____

_____

_____

_____

_____

_____

CHAPTER 10

WHY ENTREPRENEURS FAIL, AND HOW TO AVOID THE TRAPS

"To succeed, be fully committed."
—Duane Thompson

WE'VE LOOKED AT why product entrepreneurs succeed, and it's important that we look at why they fail so you can recognize the warning signs and avoid their consequences or correct them.

First, here are the top ten reasons *products* fail:

1. The entrepreneur has no passion or personal connection to the product "story."
2. The entrepreneur does not understand the target market and the branding process.
3. The product does not solve a specific problem of the target market.
4. There was no proper planning on the cost of product development.
5. The product was not tested or failed to collect feedback from prelaunch.
6. There is no plan for product scale up and growth.
7. The product packaging does not communicate positioning, identity, and values.

8. There is insufficient product funding.
9. There is a failure to develop an adequate resource and advisory team (mentorship).
10. There is a failure to track and document the product's unique success factors.

Second, here are the top ten reasons product ***entrepreneurs*** fail:

1. They think they are committed, but they really aren't.
2. They let personal problems interfere with their ability to focus on their product succeeding.
3. They lack money or resources.
4. They lack imagination.
5. They allow their pride to blind them to the benefits of constructive criticism.
6. They don't consider the advice of other product entrepreneurs.
7. They don't work with a mentor.
8. They're not willing to course correct or try something new when they see their product failing.
9. They don't work well with other people and don't try.
10. They don't give back to their communities.

To Succeed, You Must Be FULLY Committed

As you can see from the previous list, the top reason product entrepreneurs fail is lack of commitment. The story behind why you created your product may be genuinely great and you may THINK you feel passionate about seeing it succeed, but if every time you hit a bump and pothole on your way to product success you become negative and drone on about how maybe it's time to quit, then you have an attitude and, most likely, a commitment problem.

And this is a PROBLEM. Before you craft your business plan, before you test your product on consumers, before you do ANYTHING, if you feel even the smallest bit of doubt about whether you should bring a product to the marketplace, step back, dig deep down, and really ask yourself why you think you want to do this.

Though your personal reason and interest may be real, if you find your core motivation is to achieve, say, fame, or to become filthy rich, then you're probably setting yourself up for a fall. Anyone with motivations like these during product development and implementation is sure to become disappointed. If you see yourself reflected in this example, I advise you to walk away from the idea of becoming a product entrepreneur. But don't get me wrong, being famous and making tons of money are not bad outcomes of creating a successful product—they simply shouldn't be your core motivations.

It's normal to feel down when you have setbacks, such as failing to meet all your goals and timelines. More negative feedback than you anticipated can sting too. But you have to start this entrepreneur journey embracing the idea that you will allow yourself—not your emotions—to be in control of how you'll respond to the setbacks. You can feel down for a moment, but then you've got to pick yourself up.

As I mentioned earlier, always remember where you started in this journey so that you can appreciate just how far you've come, even if you haven't yet reached your destination. What may seem like failure on the surface may actually be progress when you measure it against where you could be and where you started.

This all comes down to taking responsibility for having a good attitude and staying FULLY committed to your project.

Anyone who walks away from their product after a few setbacks is not committed. I had plenty of setbacks when I was launching my salsa, but I chose to stay the course.

Commitment is not making excuses. It's finding a way to get something done even when it appears impossible. If I had stayed in my six–figure–income job, there is truly no way I could have made Asorbas what it is today. I could see Asorbas's potential, and I knew what I had to do so that it could reach it—I had to leave that high–paying job and find another, less stressful way to keep money coming in the door to give Asorbas my all. So, like I said earlier, I got a night job buffing floors—a job with little responsibility that helped me pay the bills so I could stay focused on the salsa during the day.

That's commitment! If you don't think it's in you to make major life changes to give your product a chance to succeed, then seriously consider whether you truly want to walk down the product entrepreneur path.

Here, we'll bore into the other personal obstacles that you must stay aware of and overcome in order to have a chance at succeeding.

Other Obstacles to Success

Personal Problems

Personal problems can interfere with your push to pursue your product dream, but don't let them. Of course, there are some problems—like discovering you have a serious illness, an unexpected death that may leave you devastated, a serious accident—that would prevent many of us, even the most committed, from reaching our goals, if not permanently then temporarily. But I'm speaking about another type of personal problem, like, for instance, the need to improve your income while you're working on your product launch.

Some people might feel down if they had to survive financially, like I did, by buffing floors. "Getting down" and other issues can become personal problems, but don't let them. Keep yourself "up" by working on your product. Doing this should cheer you. Remember, your product could be your ticket to self–employment.

Lacking Money

Another major reason product entrepreneurs fail is because they don't have the money, or adequate resources, to get their product off the ground. This, at any rate, is what they'd tell you. But to me, lacking money or resources is just another excuse and another sign of a lack of commitment to your supposed dream. Anyone who is serious about their product will find the money to make it happen, or they will get creative and use their imagination to *think outside the bottle* to figure out how to make it happen. Case in point, Leslie Crews.

Crews used to bottle her Kombuchick tea in recycled bottles donated to her by a cooperating business. She sanitized them then filled them with her intoxicating tea brew. She wanted to be in business, she wanted to make the tea happen, and so, she found a way. She was and is FULLY committed. And now, she's reached a new level of success that allows her to use new bottles—she no longer needs or uses recycled bottles.

Letting Your Pride Get the Best of You

If pride gets in the way of your ability to benefit from constructive criticism, then tame that pride beast. Keep front and center that criticism is intended to help you improve your product, not hurt you. If I had become upset when people told me some of my original salsa jars looked like "hair grease" containers and I had insisted on using the same jar, I wouldn't have found the success I claim today. Remember, you should be focused on improving your product, not your ego.

Ignoring the Advice of Successful Product Entrepreneurs

Some product entrepreneurs view themselves as artists, thinking one of their top priorities is to be "different from the other guy or gal." Well, one of your goals *should* be to stand out from your competition; but you can gain a lot from building alliances with other product entrepreneurs, especially successful ones who may be willing to share their business war stories to help you avoid mistakes. There is nothing wrong with friendly competition. There is nothing wrong with becoming good acquaintances with competitors either. I have taken advice from other salsa makers, and it's made my business stronger.

Failing to Work with a Mentor

I can't stress enough the importance of working closely with a mentor to help you through not only the basics of your product work but also the toughest aspects of it. Did you notice I included failure to work with a mentor on *both* the "reasons products fail" and "reasons product entrepreneurs fail" lists at the start of this chapter? Taking a mentor's advice could mean the difference between staying the course or quitting; it could be the difference between taking a few years to achieve your dream or many years, if at all. For instance, for me, Michele Hoskins is a heroine. Her advice in Asorbas's early days—to work with a turnkey manufacturer so that I could focus on selling my salsa—helped solve a lot of problems. Remember my exploding jars and too short a product shelf life? Without Michele it would have likely taken me longer to resolve those issues. Because of her, I had more time to sell the salsa, and because I had worked with a turnkey manufacturer that helped me vastly improve the salsa, I had a far stronger product to promote.

Not Willing to Course Correct

You may have a specific idea of how your product *should* be, but as I mentioned earlier in the *Playbook*, many times you'll have to change how you put your product together in order to meet a business objective. You have to be prepared for this eventuality and not be resistant to doing things differently. A resistance to course correcting could have a major negative impact on your product's bottom line. Remember how disappointed I was the first time I tried my salsa after it went through the first Mama Vida run? It would have been cost prohibitive, and frankly, almost impossible, for the manufacturer to create vast quantities of the salsa with expensive ingredients from farmers' markets and similar sources that I had been buying them from.

While you'll still have the "same" product in the end, it may be different in the details. Know from the outset that this may happen and be open to change.

Not Working Well with Other People

Just because you're likely the principal person running your business in the early days, you'll still be working with others, like your manufacturer. To be successful, you must work with them *well*. If one of the reasons you're working for yourself is because you've typically had a hard time working with others in various jobs, you have to accept that this has been a problem and work on improving it. Stay aware of this personal trap and keep in mind that you must respect others and treat them with professional courtesy at all times. If you're difficult to work with your reputation could get out and other professionals who you may need may not want to work with you.

Don't forget, YOU are your product. Every move you make reflects on it, so make the right moves.

Not Giving Back to Their Communities

If you give to your community, it will give back to you. Entrepreneurs who resist opportunities to donate small portions of their product to local events miss an opportunity to get their product and their brand name in front of new people. While it may seem like "giving" your product away, look at such events as business investments. Small investments can return big dividends in terms of sales down the road.

It All Comes Down to Knowing Yourself

To sum up, if you're committed to succeeding, to giving your product your all, you must "know thyself." Know your character and emotional weaknesses, and stay self–aware as you march down the product development path. A major weakness of mine is that I'm hard–headed. I get stuck on a way of doing things and don't want to course correct. Because I've identified this weakness, I've been able to manage it when it tries to prevent me from doing the right thing by my salsa.

Self–awareness is a key to succeeding. By being self–aware, you'll know when it's time to put up your dukes and fight off the negative demons that would prevent you from moving forward. Remember to stay positive and to *think outside the bottle*. Find new ways of thinking through old problems so that you become one of those entrepreneurs who succeed, not one of the many who fail.

**

Write down your character traits, flaws, and strengths in "Thinking Outside the Bottle," then brainstorm ways that you can improve. For example, if you're too prideful, and you let that pride get in the way of taking constructive criticism, write down "character flaw: pride gets in the way of taking constructive criticism" and "solution: stay aware of self–pride and pledge to stay open to constructive criticism and to remain mindful that it is not personal." Your pledge could also include an affirmation of staying positive: "Whenever someone delivers constructive criticism, I pledge to accept the criticism in the positive manner in which it is meant and to thank the person who is trying to help me." Remember to also write down your strengths. In down times, look back over the positive things you've said about yourself to ensure you'll stay in good spirits.

In the next chapter, we'll look at the lessons you learned in corporate America or a job elsewhere that can help you succeed as a product entrepreneur.

THINKING OUTSIDE THE BOTTLE

_____

_____

_____

_____

_____

_____

_____

_____

_____

_____

_____

_____

_____

_____

_____

_____

_____

_____

_____

_____

_____

_____

_____

_____

_____

_____

_____

_____

_____

_____

_____

_____

_____

_____

CHAPTER 11

APPLYING THE LESSONS YOU LEARNED IN CORPORATE AMERICA (OR ANOTHER JOB) TO YOUR PRODUCT VENTURE

"As I was putting my business together, I leaned on lessons I learned from all the jobs that I had worked."
—**Duane Thompson**

IN PREVIOUS CHAPTERS, I've touched on some of the lessons I learned while working in corporate America that have helped me succeed as a product entrepreneur. If you have worked for an established company, especially if you had some level of leadership responsibility there, you also have a lot of business skills and knowledge to draw from as you launch your product.

In this chapter, we'll look at the lessons you may have picked up in your previous work incarnation and how they can help you. It's good to have a checklist to remind yourself that though you may be a newbie entrepreneur, you're not a newbie businessperson. It's a confidence booster as well as an important reference as you tackle the challenges of your new work life. It's all too easy to forget what we've learned, but having this list will keep it front and center and you on your toes.

The Lesson Checklist

The lessons that follow are ones I know intimately, having learned them in my days managing construction projects and running buildings. Fiscal Management kicks off the list because it's one of the most important things you need to know to move forward in business.

Let's take a look back at what we've learned so that *you* can take steps forward in your product entrepreneur journey!

Checklist Items

☐ **Understand Fiscal Management and Financial Reports—** You *always* need to know *exactly* how your business is performing financially. If I were to ask you at this very minute what your current profit and loss picture looks like, you should be able to give the correct answer immediately. You need to know how to read profit and loss statements and net worth statements and know the status of your accounts receivable (the money purchasers owe you). In my other business life, we lived and died by those reports. In my Asorbas experience, it's been no different.

It may seem obvious that any business owner should stay on top of their company's earnings, but I've seen many entrepreneurs get so caught up in their day–to–day business that they lose sight of their bottom line. They are so busy creating and developing their product or focusing on some other aspect of the business that they fall into the red. Though I'd learned the importance of fiscal management and staying on top of financial reports in my previous jobs, in Asorbas's early days, I too got caught up in the product, the product, the product. I didn't always see the forest because I let the trees get in the way. Remember how I was losing money when I sold my salsa at the convenience store? Fortunately, when I got serious about making a real go of Asorbas, I leaned back on the lessons about fiscal management and responsibility I'd learn in my earlier jobs. This has a lot to do with why I remain in business today.

Sadly, I know former entrepreneurs who can't make the same claim. Sometimes entrepreneurs get so deep in the red that they truly can't recover. I'm thinking of a father–and–son team that financed their business on the back of the dad's Social Security check. In the process of trying to establish their business, they lost sight of what was going on with their bottom line, and by the time they came to me for advice, it truly was too late to do anything. Their business folded. Financially, they were professionally *and* personally devastated.

So again, make staying on top of your profit and loss statements a top priority every step of the way.

- ☐ **Understand Peer Business–to–Business Relationships—** To have a strong relationship with your customers (remember that in product entrepreneurland, your customers are the organizations you do business with), you need to get to know them. You need to understand who they are as people, their business experience, and how they believe they can help you sell your product. When I was working for the construction company, I researched the companies we were working with, learned who the top associates were, and made sure I was on a first–name basis with them. In phone calls and e–mails, I related to them first as people, congratulating them on birthdays, the birth of their children, and other significant life events. I made sure to share a bit of the personal joy milestones of my life as well. Then I got down to business. We were all on a first–name basis and related as people and businesspeople. Approaching business this way builds trust, a critical commodity you want to nurture if you're going to succeed.

- ☐ **Know and Respect Your Customer's Concerns—**Once, on a construction project I was overseeing, the building's future business tenants made it clear they didn't want our construction debris falling on the nearby streets. They didn't want passing cars to pick up nails and other construction castoffs, so I made their concern a top priority. In addition to constructing a safe, smart building, I ensured we kept the surrounding area as clean as possible. Unfortunately, at the helm of Sabrosa Foods, I once forgot the critical lesson of knowing and respecting my customer's concern, and I paid dearly for it. I authorized a salsa shipment to a store, not taking care to check the store's product–delivery acceptance times. The shipment arrived outside their product–acceptance window, so they rejected our delivery. We had paid $700 for the delivery and wound up having to pay another $700 the next day, when the driver returned within the accepted time frame. It was a fee that we had to pay, because we had to get the product on the shelves or we'd have lost far more than the additional delivery–fee charge.

The store hadn't made me aware of the delivery window, but I should have made it my business to know it. Make it your business to know your customer's business and their concerns, because it all comes back on you anyway.

☐ **Be Diligent and Persistent**—Always, always, always follow up on all business–related matters. Always make sure every aspect of your business is performing correctly, from accounts receivable to the on–time delivery of your product to store shelves. Don't let anything fall through the cracks. On your calendar, schedule a series of business checks to make on a recurring basis and stick with them.

☐ **Manage Time Wisely**—Make a schedule for all tasks to be performed and stick with it. This will keep you honest, help you stick to and juggle multiple tasks, and move you more efficiently toward your goals.

☐ **Think Creatively**—As they say, when life gives you lemons, make lemonade. Apply the same practice in business. When I learned another company wanted Sabrosa Foods to discontinue using the Sabrosa name for our salsa, instead of waging a costly legal fight, I chose to *think outside the bottle,* and the new name, Asorbas, was born.

☐ **Develop Resources, Develop a Team**—Everyone you meet along your product entrepreneur journey is a potential resource. Always be sure to have business cards on hand. Give them out and collect them. Follow up with an e–mail or phone call. Let the person know you enjoyed meeting them. Stay in touch with updates about how your business is going, and ask them about their business. Someday, you're going to need their help.

While many of you are probably going it alone at this point, as your business grows you will probably have to put together a team to power you forward. Ultimately, you will need an attorney, an accountant, possibly an office manager and other support staff. You may not have the financial means to have these professionals on staff now, but you should already be identifying who they may be. I didn't have an attorney when I started out, but I befriended several over the course of attending business functions, luncheons, and training events as I was getting into the thick of Sabrosa. I shared with them where I was trying to take my company, and they offered me information pro bono. Now I work with one of those attorneys exclusively. He's on retainer.

☐ **Even if You're the Leader, Be a Team Player**—You can't do everything in your business. Once you have an established team, you need to delegate tasks so that you can focus on the big picture; but also be sure to make employees know that they are as equally important to your operation as you are.

☐ **Exercise Leadership Skills**—Real leaders inspire others to "get the job done." Do this by leading by example. Everything you ask others to do, you have to let them know you've "been there" or are willing to do it too.

☐ **Create a Positive Business Environment**—It's important to set a positive tone and corporate philosophy before your business grows and gets big. This gets baked into your business's culture, and the goodness grows as the company grows. Nothing is better than seeing smiling faces even on days when business is not the best. It keeps people up and ready to do business.

☐ **Know How to Relax**—It's not good to do nothing but work on your product. You have to pace yourself. In the early days of devoting myself to Sabrosa, I made sure to schedule one day a week where I would do nothing—that's right, *nothing*—but relax and meditate. TV and radio were off the agenda. I needed this one day to recharge myself so I wouldn't stop running.

☐ **Communicate Effectively**—An effective leader is an effective communicator. You must always ensure that your message and instructions are correctly understood by staff and customers. Do this by asking them to repeat what you said to them to ensure you communicated well.

☐ **Stay Healthy While Running Your Business**—During my corporate America days, I didn't always pay attention to my health. I skipped routine checkups and didn't always exercise and eat right. I got sick and my productivity plummeted. Being my own boss at Sabrosa, though, I literally cannot afford to get sick. So as the president and CEO, I've always made sure to see the doctor for regular checkups, keep to a steady gym schedule, and maintain a healthy diet. When you own a business, you *are* your business. If your business is going to stay healthy, *you* have to stay healthy.

☐ **Go Above and Beyond**—As the lifeblood of your company, you have to be prepared to go the extra mile every day you step into the office. Here's an example that piggybacks off an earlier one in this chapter: What if the freight company I work with had been unable to redeliver my salsas to the store the next day, after I had sent them to make a delivery outside of the accepted delivery time? If that had happened, I would have delivered my product myself the next day. That means I would have rented as many U–Hauls as it took, enlisted a bunch of dollies, and paid employees and professional moving people to do a lot of tugging and lifting, and then been on my way to pick up my salsas from the freight company and pack them for store delivery. That's going the extra mile to make sure you stay in business.

☐ **Analyze**—Look at a situation, run it through your head, and foresee the outcomes. If a particular way of conducting business led to a negative outcome previously, why repeat it? One definition of crazy is not changing your actions even though they repeatedly lead to a negative outcome. Don't be that person in business.

☐ **Don't Trip Over Dimes to Get to the Dollars**—You have to pay to do business. Don't let what may seem like a steep cost, like the $700 I double–paid to the freight company to redeliver the salsa, prevent you from making things happen. Fees for moving product and for other items and needs may seem hefty, but compare them to your product's earning potential. Remember, the fees are an investment. I may have double–paid the $700, but at the end of the day, I made a large profit on the sales of that particular shipment of salsa. So don't trip over the dimes if you want to make the dollars!

Last, but not least . . .

☐ **Know When to Cut Bait**—If you've followed all the steps in *Think Outside the Bottle* and find there is no market for your product, then face facts and accept that you can't put a round peg into a square hole. Your financial statements and the feedback you receive from consumers during your product's testing phase should help you know whether it's time to move on. Also, if you're severely behind deadlines for achieving critical goals and cannot, after careful analysis, see how you will reach them in a reasonable amount of time, then you may need to decide whether to cut bait and abandon your product.

**

In "Thinking Outside the Bottle," write down the business lessons you've already learned and brainstorm how you can use them to help you succeed.

In the next chapter, we'll look at how being open to new ways of conducting your product business could mean big business gains for you.

THINKING OUTSIDE THE BOTTLE

_____

_____

_____

_____

_____

_____

_____

_____

_____

_____

CHAPTER 12

WHEN OPPORTUNITY KNOCKS, THINK OUTSIDE THE BOTTLE

"Business IS relationships."
—Duane Thompson

YOU MAY NOT realize it, but you've been building the foundation for new business opportunities since you drew up your product's business plan, and probably even before that. You started building this foundation when you began establishing relationships. People you know from as far back as grade school could play a role in the next phase of your—and your product's—story.

You see, I fervently believe that in business, strong relationships are most important. Having supporters speaks volumes about your capacity to grow your business. These relationships could unexpectedly present you great opportunities you never even thought to put in your business plan. And when this happens, I advise you to go off your plan and take a shot at the unexpected.

But don't just wait for an unexpected opportunity. After a few years of getting into a selling groove, actively pursue new opportunities. You have to grow to stay in the selling game.

I know it takes a lot to be a product entrepreneur, but on top of all your other commitments, to better position yourself for new opportunities, from the get–go you should:

- **Nurture Your Relationships**—Nurture your old business connections and personal relationships. Keep in touch through a few phone calls or e–mails a year and send cards for the major holidays. When you can, meet face to face. If you don't establish, harbor, and nurture relationships, you won't do business for long.

- **Stay Engaged in Your Community**—However small, take a role in a community service initiative. As I mentioned in Chapter 7, every year Sabrosa Foods donates its salsa to the local foodbank. This helps the community and also exposes Asorbas to new consumers. One of the beautiful things about giving back is that sometimes you get back what you give.

- **Give Back to Youth**—Even if it's something as simple as letting one young person shadow you at work for a day, you've done a lot. And you never know—that young person could one day be working with you or might shed some light on new ways your product might click with the younger generation.

- **Stay Involved with Your College Alma Mater**—Be active in alumni groups. This could simply mean attending the annual holiday gathering held by the local alumni chapter of your university. If you live in the same area as your old school, get a seat on a board and have a say.

- **Meet New People**—Go out of your way to make new connections. Find an association, club, or professional development group that's right for you. If you're low on cash and can't pay dues, check whether and when the organization may hold a free, open meeting. Engage in conversations. Give and collect business cards. Take members up on offers to play golf, tennis, jog. You never know where these relationships will lead in business.

My (Other) Story

I've done everything I just suggested you do: I've employed high school students in cooperation with a local youth program; helped students in a business project at a local high school; mentored entrepreneurs at my local Small Business Development Center; and given back to my community in a number of other ways. But for reasons that will become obvious, meeting new people has been especially important to the evolution of Sabrosa Foods. First, let me say that the evolution was not by design. It happened as result of me dating a Hampton–area college student. The relationship didn't last, but it led to a watershed moment for my company that paved the path to a business dream I didn't even know I had.

I'm going to take you on a trip, where I'll show you how staying involved in outside pursuits, meeting new people, and nurturing relationships can help your business flourish. Think of yourself as a backseat passenger in a car with three other people, me and this play's other stars: Dr. Clinton Turner, the state of Virginia's former commissioner of agriculture and a Virginia State University grad, and William Crutchfield, a retired US Department of Agriculture official. Like me and Dr. Turner, Crutchfield is also a VSU alum. Everyone takes his turn telling you about their role in the life of a certain salsa as we travel along memory lane.

I'm taking my time behind the wheel of a four–door sedan when Dr. Turner pipes up: "I met Duane after he left Virginia State University—being a VSU graduate, we connected. I don't remember what the social setting was, but anyway, when someone comes up to you and says they make salsa, you stop and look at them and you say 'You make what?' So he said it again—'I make salsa.' I asked him, 'Why the hell do you make that?' I mean really, how many people do you run into who tell you they make salsa?"

Behind the wheel, I chuckle. "Actually, I met Dr. Turner because I was dating a relative of his. I told him my story—about how my grandmother taught me how to garden and how I came to make the salsa. You know, my acid reflux issues and all. Then Dr. Turner encouraged me to set up an exhibit at the Virginia State Fair. I sold my salsa there and competed against other foods from local vendors for a state prize, and my salsa won the Director's Choice Award."

Says Turner, "When I heard Duane's story, I thought *maybe more of us should have remembered what our grandparents taught us and capitalize on it.* Anyway, I tasted the salsa at the state fair, and I thought it was great. I knew I wanted to help Duane out. We started buying it and shipping it around to a lot of our friends. We would go to the store and ask for it. I would encourage my friends to go to the store and ask for it. At that time I think many of my friends would go to the stores and would order it for gifts and birthdays. My wife would eat one jar at a time by herself, and to this day we're still using his product. Anyway, one day I called up Crutchfield."

Crutchfield is sitting in the backseat right behind me. He's somewhat younger than Turner, who actually mentored Crutchfield when he was a youngster. For decades, the two have kept up a friendship.

"It was sometime in 2009, the year I retired from the USDA," Crutchfield says. "Dr. Turner had me over at his house and offered me some salsa and told me it was made by a VSU grad. I tried it and thought it was very, very good! There was no doubt about it. Next thing I know, Dr. Turner was saying to me, 'Crutchfield, with your connections, do you think you could get Duane's salsa into the military commissaries? So I started talking to some of my friends and made contact with some people at the Fort Lee commissary headquarters, and they put me in touch with a buyer. So I arranged for Duane and myself to meet her and have a tasting."

I continue driving the car down memory lane and recall that meeting. "I pitched the product at the defense commissary at Fort Lee, right outside VSU. The buyer thought it would be a great product and would do well. I told her that considering our production capabilities, we could line shelves in seven or eight stores. She said, 'Duane, we don't put products in something as low as that many stores. The test is something like thirty stores. If you're not willing to go into thirty stores, our business is done here.' I said, 'OK, we'll go into thirty stores.' I had no idea how I was going to produce that much product. I didn't even have the money to do it. I just committed myself to it. I was forced to put up or shut up."

Says Crutchfield, "Around the time I met Duane, he signed a nondisclosure agreement with my consulting firm, TWC and Associates, for general help with his business. We helped Duane get the military contract in hand in early 2010. Here comes along Duane with a very unique product, but the only thing that wasn't jiving was his lack of capital and the way the commissary did business. They dealt directly with a large grocery buyer, who had the budget to supply the commissary, which, like Duane pretty much said, he didn't have. The commissary did have a mechanism in place back then to do it the way Duane wanted to do it, however, but it was an uphill battle all the way."

"Yeah, I had to get creative with the financing," I say. "I went back with the project in my hand, and it was like, alright I have a federal government contract in hand, signed and delivered. I went on Google and learned about something called a factoring broker. Basically, they front money for you to put your product in a store. I was in a fight or flight situation. Do I run or do I fight? At that moment I knew I wasn't going to run. I had people behind me who helped me get this meeting, and I wasn't going to fail, so I chose to fight. Fortunately, I found a factoring broker that loaned me the money to get into the thirty stores. But there were other hurdles too, like getting all that salsa into all those stores. I didn't have the financial resources to distribute everywhere, and I certainly hadn't agreed to a distribution plan that far ranging with my manufacturer. Well, thank goodness for having friends."

Crutchfield interjects, "We liked Duane, and we wanted to help him succeed. I remember personally delivering four or five cases of salsa to Fort Lee. Supplying the product and putting it on the shelves yourself is out of the norm, but that's what Duane had to do initially. Between myself and some other associates, we worked with Duane for three years. It was a lot of miles, a lot of phone calls, a lot of begging. We worked with him for a nominal fee. I guess the moral of this story if that if you have a product that's good, you need to make connections and network to take your product to the next level."

"That's the truth!" I say as I ease the car into a parking spot.

The Commissaries

In May 2011, Asorbas made its way onto thirty defense commissary shelves below Canada, as far west as Fort Knox, Kentucky, as far south as Fort Bragg, North Carolina, and all the way up the East Coast. While I received much needed help from Crutchfield to distribute it, I pretty much drove to and stocked every commissary myself, which I now think is crazy. I would never do that again; and with the money Sabrosa Foods is making now, I don't have to.

As of late 2015, Asorbas was being sold in fifty–two commissaries in the same geographic commissary sales loop it had covered in 2011—a 73 percent commissary distribution jump. Today, about 30 percent of Asorbas's sales come from the commissaries. The other 40 percent comes from wholesale and other retailers' shelves. (This does not include Farm Fresh, however. That contract ended around the time my salsa entered the commissaries because my distributor to Farm Fresh went out of business.) As for the rest of Asorbas's sales, 20 percent comes from events and 10 percent comes from online.

Before Dr. Turner and Crutchfield entered my life, I had never considered the commissaries. I had been so wrapped up in trying to see the salsa succeed in regular retail stores—what I thought, at the time, defined success. It took my two friends to show me that this was not the only way.

Through my experience with them, I have discovered that you should always be willing to go outside your comfort zone. If you're not open to new things, you won't learn what else you can do . . . and you may be surprised by what you're capable of achieving.

Thanks to these two men, Sabrosa Foods was put on a path to enter its most lucrative phase yet, but that journey was not easy. As a struggling entrepreneur, you have to be prepared to pivot. When you deviate from your original business plan to try something new, you'll have to reconfigure your business costs in terms of dollars and time all over again. It will probably mean that you will need more than your original budget to make things happen.

Turning the Ship Around

Because my business was small, I quickly adapted to working with the commissaries. It doesn't take as long to turn a small ship around as it does a large one, but it still requires a big effort.

And for me, this meant making a bigger financial investment in my salsa.

Prior to meeting Dr. Turner and Crutchfield, about 70 percent of my capital came from manufacturing and selling my salsa in small batches. In Asorbas's early years, I ate what I killed. I couldn't do any more than that. So when that day came when the commissary said, "Yeah, we'll take this," I had to ramp up my business tenfold. To make this happen, I borrowed about 30 percent of what I needed from friends, including Crutchfield and Dr. Turner, and family. The other 70 percent came from my personal savings and salsa sales proceeds.

Fortunately, Asorbas netted about $10,000 from its first commissary sales run, and I was able to pay my friends, family, and the factor back. And eventually, with Crutchfield and Dr. Turner's help, I was able to pay a broker to help me fill the commissaries.

So while I adapted to change quickly because my operation was small, the relationships I established, harbored, and nurtured are the main reason I successfully navigated the commissary sales opportunity.

Sabrosa Foods's Most Lucrative Days Ever

Asorbas's successful commissary sales opened up a critical opportunity with the military—another opportunity that I had not foreseen. After two years selling the salsa at Fort Lee, Sabrosa Foods was approached with an offer to provide services—yes, services—to the military. Specifically, they asked whether I was interested in providing a full-service cooking staff to serve military personnel at Langley Air Force Base—the very base I had left a lucrative job behind several years before to pursue selling salsa full time.

As for their question: Heck, yeah, I wanted to serve the personnel. I was ready to adapt to and learn something new. I was thinking, *Yeah, let this thing go where it's going to go. Why stop with the commissary?*

How can I do more business with the Department of Defense?

That was in 2013. As of 2016, Sabrosa Foods has six military contracts from which we gross about $6 million annually, and the company has picked up two additional full–service federal food contracts. And Asorbas? Its bottom line sales have tripled since 2009. In addition to the commissaries, Asorbas is sold in multiple retail stores along the East Coast, in Canada, Trinidad and Tobago, Zambia, and at www.sabrosafoods.com. You'll find it in mom–and–pop gourmet stores, health–food chains, and food service companies, which serve it to several Hampton Roads universities and military dining facilities.

Most of this was not in my original business plan—remember how I said that business plans are living documents? Well, you can also think of them as drafts that can and *should* undergo continued editing and refinement, but unlike a book that becomes a "final," your business plan's final chapter is *never* written until you hand the reigns of your company over to someone else and retire.

But there's one thing your plan should always state, no matter if you're at the start or end of your game: To win, always *think outside the bottle*.

**

Use "Thinking Outside the Bottle" to brainstorm new sales opportunities for your product. You may want to keep this section blank for a few months, or even years, as you get your bearings in the initial stages of developing your product and establishing it in the marketplace. But remember, you can come back to the *Playbook* over and over for refresher courses and to take new notes. Use the section below when you're ready.

Next up, we'll ponder your business and personal life in the future.

THINKING OUTSIDE THE BOTTLE

_____

_____

_____

_____

_____

_____

_____

_____

_____

_____

_____

_____

_____

_____

_____

_____

_____

_____

_____

_____

_____

_____

_____

_____

_____

_____

_____

_____

_____

_____

_____

_____

_____

_____

CONCLUSION

HAVING VISION—SEEING YOUR BUSINESS (AND YOUR LIFE) IN THE FUTURE

"There is a natural progression of getting from here to there. It's profound: Verbalize it, speak it, think it, and nine times out of ten it will become a reality."
—Duane Thompson

A LITTLE OVER ten years ago, you could only find Duane's Holiday Salsa at a small convenience/deli store in Rockville, Maryland. Today, after having undergone four name changes (at one point, I called it "Duane's Gourmet Salsa"), two manufacturers, and expanding to an offering of four salsa variations, you can purchase it in stores along the East Coast and overseas. I've gone from losing money on Asorbas to it turning a very healthy profit.

I don't want to sound arrogant, but to tell the truth I saw this coming. Back when I was mixing salsa in my Maryland home to keep up with demand at my friend's store, I just had a feeling that was only the start if only I had the guts to give the salsa my all. After doing a gut check, I knew I indeed had what it would take to make Asorbas succeed.

Leaving my six–figure–income job helped me focus almost completely on my salsa business, and it had another positive impact: It removed any sort of safety net that could have prevented me from making Asorbas all it could be. Remember in Chapter 1 when I said failure was not an option? Because I'd left my job, I didn't have much income coming through the door, save for my savings and the bit of money I was making buffing floors, so Asorbas *had* to make it. Removing that safety net helped it succeed.

Today, salsa sales account for a third of my company's income, and the rest comes from the services we provide to the federal government. With the federal contracts came another major change: Sabrosa, which had started off with me as the sole employee, is now nearly 120 employees strong!

And here's where things get interesting: Just as I could see Asorbas's potential more than ten years ago, I can see where I'd like it and Sabrosa Foods to be another fifteen or twenty years from now.

To get what I'm about to say, remember that Sabrosa Foods is the parent company under which Asorbas is sold.

Hang with me.

I know you've heard about companies creating and producing a product, then selling it to another company to keep it in the marketplace. That's what I intend to do with Asorbas.

I see it as the go–to brand for nachos. I envision selling it to a large conglomerate for placement in markets all over the US, if not the world. Sabrosa Foods would no longer control the product, but we'd still receive revenue from its sales.

So what would happen to Sabrosa Foods? It will likely sell other products, but will mainly be a dynamic service business.

Wait, you're saying, how can the man who started off *Think Outside the Bottle* by pushing the idea that the US needs more product entrepreneurs now be telling me his goal is to helm a service–centered business?

The reason is less hypocritical than you may be thinking. I see Sabrosa as the go–to source for Americans seeking to create and sell products.

The endgame for me is to help people and to give back.

Sabrosa will be a funnel through which product entrepreneurs travel to reach their goals and find success. They'll receive one–on–one help, from being taught how to develop their story to how to develop and sell their product, and everything that comes in between—and after—those steps. There will be a cost, but the service won't be cost prohibitive. As a reader of *Think Outside the Bottle*, you've only gotten a taste of what Sabrosa can and will do for you.

Leslie Crews, who has found success with Kombuchick, has been our beta test. When I see her eyes glow because she's landed great media coverage for her tea or when her sales have exceeded her expectations, a fire lights up in me too. I'm passionate about seeing others succeed in the product game. I want you to succeed. You have to succeed. I want to help you get there!

Part of being an entrepreneur is identifying and seizing opportunities that can take your business to the next level. After my company landed the military service contract, I had a little room to ponder other business opportunities. So when I recognized I had a real passion for working with product entrepreneurs and for seeing this country expand production again, I knew establishing this service business was in the cards.

That's where I plan to take my product business, and any smart entrepreneur should be thinking about their endgame as well. You don't want to work forever, so you must have an exit strategy. Let your product give to others as you give back to yourself; let it enable you to take days, weeks, months, years lounging on the beach, exploring new hobbies, traveling to foreign countries for pleasure, and buying things you want and having the time to enjoy them. Let it allow you to have the luxury to spend solid time with friends and family, which for me now includes my beautiful, smart–as–a–whip wife, Lingisi, and my toddler son, Duane Jr. Yes, it's about having the time to truly enjoy your golden years.

So in this next phase of Sabrosa Foods's journey, I hope over the next twenty or so years to help many entrepreneurs give birth to US–made products. And when the time is right, I'll hang up my apron and take the time, finally, to truly enjoy the world we've all made together.

THINKING OUTSIDE THE BOTTLE

Now that you've worked through the entire *Playbook*, use the following pages to write down additional notes (for example, web addresses, potential mentors' phone numbers, and business budget numbers), your ideas, and even questions that you'd like to ask me. You can e–mail me at duane@sabrosafoods.com.

But the *Playbook* doesn't end here. Keep going to find the bonus quiz, "Are You Ready to Become a Product Entrepreneur?," worksheets to help you master calculating sales markups, sales margins, and product cost, and bonus Asorbas recipes!

Here's to *thinking outside the bottle*. Cheers!

_____

_____

_____

_____

_____

_____

_____

_____

_____

_____

_____

_____

_____

_____

_____

_____

_____

_____

_____

_____

_____

_____

_____

_____

_____

_____

_____

_____

_____

_____

_____

_____

_____

_____

_____

_____

_____

_____

_____

_____

_____

_____

_____

_____

_____

_____

_____

_____

_____

_____

_____

_____

_____

_____

_____

_____

_____

_____

_____

_____

_____

_____

_____

BONUS: QUIZ

ARE YOU READY TO BECOME A PRODUCT ENTREPRENEUR?

1. Do you want to create and sell a product simply to make money?

    a) Yes
    b) No

2. Do you have a personal tie to the product you want to create—for instance, does it solve a problem that you deal with, or is it something you've always dreamed of having?

    a) Yes
    b) No

3. Have you considered what financial resources it will take to create and launch a product into the marketplace, and can you be capable of financing the venture?

    a) Yes
    b) No

4. Will you have or seek support from businesses, family members, friends, professionals, or others to assist with your product business?

    a) Yes
    b) No

5. Are you aware of your character strengths and flaws?

    a) Yes
    b) No

6. Do you take constructive criticism well?

    a) Yes
    b) No

7. Will you work with a mentor as you navigate the product entrepreneur route?

    a) Yes
    b) No

8. Are you willing to give your product business everything you have—your blood, sweat, and tears—to see it succeed?

    a) Yes
    b) No

9. Is the product idea not yours, but someone else's dream (a parent's, spouse's, friend's) even if you have a personal tie to the product idea?

    a) Yes
    b) No

10. Generally speaking, are you open to adapting and course correcting? In other words, are you highly open to change?

    a) Yes
    b) No

ANSWER KEY

1) B
2) A
3) A
4) A
5) A
6) A
7) A
8) A
9) B
10) A

If you answered all ten questions correctly, hone your story and get that business plan written! If you answered at least eight questions correctly, you are probably ready to start working on making your product idea a reality, though I'd advise you to examine the questions you answered wrong and work on course correcting before you get too far.

If you answered seven or fewer questions right, and you do not believe you are committed to making the changes necessary to come up with the correct answers, then take a deep look at yourself and your motivations for launching a product. This is probably not the right time for you to move forward. Being a product entrepreneur requires a serious commitment. You've got to keep a smile on your face as you roll with the punches, because there will be many punches.

WORKSHEETS

The following worksheets will help you master calculating sales markups, sales margins, and product cost. Refer back to Chapter 5: "The Product Development Playbook," for more information on product cost, markups, and margins.

Calculating a Sales Markup

Directions: Use what you have learned about sales markups to answer the following questions.

1. Wholesale Price = $7
   Sales Price = $7.84
   Calculate Here:

   _____
   _____
   _____

   _____

   What is the markup? _____

2. Wholesale Price = $45
    Sales Price = $78.75
    Calculate Here:

    _____

    _____

    _____

    _____

    What is the markup? _____

3. Wholesale Price = $567.75
    Sales Price = $766.45
    Calculate Here:

    _____

    _____

    _____

    _____

    What is the markup? _____

Calculating a Sales Margin

1. Wholesale Price: $125/ Sales Price: $165
    Profit: $40
    Calculate Here:

    _____

    _____

    _____

    _____

    What is the sales margin? _____

2. Wholesale Price: $52.50/ Sales Price: $83.80
    Profit:$31.30
    Calculate Here:

    _____

    _____

    _____

    _____

    What is the sales margin? _____

3. Wholesale Price: $2,359/ Sales Price: $4,563
    Profit: $2,204
    Calculate Here:

    _____

    _____

    _____

    _____

    What is the sales margin? _____

ANSWER KEY:

1) 24.24%

2) 37.35%

3) 48.3%

Product Cost Worksheet Example

This product cost worksheet example will help you analyze your own product cost and profit.

							Explanation Notes
Product: Salsa							
Batch Size (units)				100			Enter the number of units you plan to manufacture.
Materials:							
Qty	**Materials**	**Cost**	**Shipping**	**Other**	**Total**	**Per Item**	Enter each material component
		$	$	$	$	$	separately. Qty and materials columns are descriptive only.
100	Jars	122.00			122.00		
100	Lids	40.00	1.00		41.00		Enter the cost of each component as the
100	Labels	0.11			0.11		total for the required quantity.
60 gal.	Salsa Mixture	42.00			42.00		Enter shipping costs incurred on sourcing
100	Safety Bands	1.00			1.00		components. Include packaging
Batch Total:					206.11		materials as a separate component.
Production Costs:		**Cost**	**Shipping**	**Other**			This includes all production costs with
Process		$	$	$			an identifiable and quantifiable cost.
Filling Cost		1.00			1.00		e.g. Filling costs, studio time, equipment hire, etc.
Batch Total					1.00		Include the costs of any subcontracted processes.
							Enter any shipping costs involved in sub-contracted processes.

		Total	Per Item	
		$	$	
Total Production Cost:		207.11	2.07	
Time:				
	Hours to make product	4.00		Total time to manufacture and package
	Hourly rate	15.00		Target hourly rate for your labor. This should never be below the minimum wage.
	Total time cost to produce product batch	60.00	.60	
Profitability:				
	Suggested Retail Price (SRP)	8.00	8.00	The final price to the retail consumer
	Retail Margin	33%		% retail margin to be retained by the retailer
	Trade Price		5.36	The price at which you will sell to a retailer
	Total material/time cost		2.67	The total cost of materials, production costs, and your making time (from above)
	Profit Contribution (before overheads)		2.69	The profit retained by you after deducting all costs, but excluding overheads
	Profit Contribution		50.17%	The profit contribution expressed as a percentage of the sales received by you

BONUS

ASORBAS RECIPES

Asorbas Honey–Glazed Salmon with Corn and Roasted Bell Pepper Salsa

Ingredients

3 ears of corn, shucked
2 tomatoes, peeled, seeded. and chopped
2 cups Asorbas bell pepper salsa
2 tbsp. chopped fresh flat leaf parsley
Ingredients for the salmon:
1/2 cup honey
2 tbsp. balsamic vinegar
1 tbsp. plus 2 tsp. vegetable oil
6 center–cut salmon fillets with skin
   intact, each 6 to 8 oz.
Salt and freshly ground pepper. to taste

Instructions

1. Fire up the grill.
2. Place the corn on the grill rack 5 to 6 inches from the fire and cook about 10 minutes, turning often, until the kernels have softened and are lightly browned.
3. Let cool completely. Cut off the kernels from each ear with a sharp knife, cutting the length of the ear and rotating it with each cut.
4. In a large bowl, combine the corn kernels, Asorbas bell pepper salsa (mild or medium), stir well, add salt, and pepper to taste.

5. Cover and refrigerate. Stir in the parsley just before serving.

6. To prepare the salmon, in a small saucepan stir together the honey, balsamic vinegar, and 1 tbsp. of vegetable oil.

7. Bring to a boil over high heat, reduce the heat to medium–low and cook 2 to 3 minutes, stirring often, until reduced by half.

8. In a heavy, large nonstick fry pan over medium–high heat, warm the 2 tsp. vegetable oil. Season the salmon with salt and pepper and place, skin side down, in the pan.

9. Brush the tops generously with the honey mixture and cook for 5 minutes.

10. Turn the salmon over and brush again with the honey mixture.

11. For 5 to 7 minutes, cook, turning occasionally and brushing with the honey mixture, until the salmon is glazed and opaque throughout.

12. Transfer to warmed individual plates.

13. Pass the salsa around the table and enjoy!

Asorbas Baked Salsa Chicken

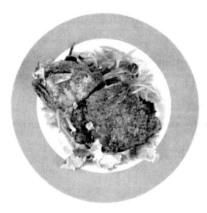

Ingredients
2 large bone–in or boneless skinless chicken
  breasts (about 1/2 lb.)
2 teaspoons taco seasoning mix
  (from 1 oz. package)
1/2 cup Asorbas mild bell pepper salsa
1/2 cup shredded cheddar cheese (2 oz.) (optional)
1 tbsp. sour cream (optional)

Instructions
1. Heat oven to 375°F. Sprinkle both sides of chicken breast with taco seasoning mix; place in ungreased 8–inch–square (2–qt.) glass baking dish. Pour salsa over chicken.
2. Bake 25 to 35 minutes or until chicken is fork tender and juices run clear. Sprinkle cheese evenly over chicken; bake 3 to 5 minutes longer or until cheese is melted. Serve with sour cream.
3. Best served with fresh garden salad accompaniment with light vinaigrette dressing.

Asorbas Party Shrimp Cocktail

Ingredients
1/2 cup of Asorbas medium bell pepper
   salsa
9 tbsp. chopped peeled ripe avocado
2 tbsp. chopped fresh basil
1/2 tsp. sugar
15 jumbo peeled and deveined tail–on
   shrimp (about 1 lb.)

Instructions
1. Combine first ingredients (through sugar) in a medium bowl; cover and chill.
2. Combine shrimp and above ingredients in a large zip–top plastic bag; seal and shake to coat shrimp.
3. Marinate in refrigerator 30 minutes.
4. Heat oil in a large nonstick skillet over medium–high heat. Remove shrimp from bag; discard marinade.
5. Add shrimp to pan; Cook 1 minute on each side or until shrimp are done.
6. Spoon 1/3 cup salsa into each of 6 martini glasses; place 5 shrimp on rim of each glass.
7. Garnish each glass with a lime wedge, if desired.

Asorbas Sweet Potato Soup

Ingredients

1 cup Asorbas mild bell pepper salsa
3 medium sweet potatoes (about 1 lb.),
   peeled and cubed
3 cups chicken or vegetable broth
1 bay leaf
1/2 tsp. dried basil
1/4 tsp. salt (optional)

Instructions

1. In a soup pot over medium heat, add broth and potatoes and let them simmer, covered, for 30 minutes, or until potatoes are tender. Cool slightly.
2. Place half of sweet potato and half of stock mixture in a blender.
3. Remove center piece of blender lid (to allow steam to escape); secure lid on blender.
4. Place a clean towel over opening in blender lid (to avoid splatters); blend until smooth.
5. Repeat procedure with remaining sweet potato and stock mixture.
6. Return mixture to soup pot, slowly stir in mild Asorbas salsa and basil. Simmer over low heat for 15 minutes.
7. Pour soup into a large bowl. Stir in salt. Divide soup evenly among 6 bowls and garnish with bay leaf, if desired.

Asorbas Peach Chutney Muffins

Ingredients

1/2 cup flour

3/4 tsp. salt

1/2 tsp. baking soda

1/4 cup light brown sugar

2 eggs, well beaten

1/2 cup oil

1/2 tsp. vanilla

1/4 cup chopped almonds
   (optional)

2 cups Asorbas Peach Chutney

Instructions

1. Preheat oven to 350°F. Lightly grease muffin tins or greased/floured 9-inch by 5-inch bread loaf pan.
2. In a large mixing bowl, combine the flour, salt, baking soda, and sugar.
3. Make a well in the center; add the eggs, oil, and vanilla and stir just until dry mixture is moistened.
4. Stir in almonds, if using them.
5. Stir in the Asorbas Peach Chutney.
6. Pour about 1/3 cup of batter into the muffin tins. Bake at 350°F for 20–25 minutes or until toothpick test is successful.
7. If baking in the loaf pan, bake at 350°F for 1 hour or until done.

Asorbas Sizzling Vegetable Fajitas

Ingredients

1 cup Asorbas Jalapeño Relish for
 sizzling sauce

1/4 cup diced tomato for sizzling
 sauce

1/4 cup onion, finely diced for
 sizzling sauce

3 tbsp. lemon juice for sizzling
 sauce

1 1/2 tbsp. fresh cilantro, finely chopped for sizzling sauce

8 oz. chopped cilantro for pesto sauce

3 garlic cloves for pesto sauce

1/2 cup olive oil for pesto sauce

1/8 tsp. salt for pesto sauce

1/8 tsp. pepper for pesto sauce

2 oz. freshly grated parmesan cheese for pesto sauce

1 medium onion, sliced

1/2 tbsp. margarine cups of combination carrots or 2 cups zucchini or 2
          cups summer squash, cut julienne style broccoli or cauliflower,
          cut into small florets or green peppers or mushrooms, thinly
          sliced or snow peas

1/2 whole lemon juice of flour tortilla warmed lime wedge for garnish

guacamole for condiment

sour cream for condiment

shredded cheddar cheese for condiment

To Make Sizzling Sauce

1. Combine all ingredients specified for sizzling sauce.
2. Let sit for at least a half hour so flavors will blend.

To Make Pesto

1. Put cilantro and garlic in a food processor and process until finely chopped.
2. With machine on, gradually add olive oil. Season and blend in cheese.

To Make Filling

1. Slice enough onion to equal about 1/2 cup. Sauté with margarine in a small cast–iron skillet over medium–high heat.
2. Cook past translucent stage until browned, about 6 to 8 minutes.
3. Prepare about 2 cups of vegetables (the combination depends on personal taste).
4. Cook all vegetables except mushrooms in lemon juice and 2 tbsp. of pesto over medium to medium–high heat.
5. When almost at al dente stage, add sliced mushrooms.
6. Continue cooking for about 1 minute.
7. The remaining pesto can be refrigerated or frozen for future use.
8. Place vegetable mixture over sizzling onions, then spoon vegetable/onion mixture into center of warmed tortillas.
9. Top with additional Asorbas relish and condiments to taste, then roll up tortillas.
10. Three tortillas make one very generous portion.

ACKNOWLEDGMENTS

For the birth of *Think Outside the Bottle: The Product Entrepreneur's Playbook*, I thank God first and foremost for instilling in me the power to believe in my passion and pursue my dreams. I could never have done this without the faith I have in you, the Almighty.

I also thank my family for supporting yet another challenge that cut into our time together. I am especially grateful to my brilliant and beautiful wife, Lingisi, without whom I would not have come so far. She always comforts and consoles, never complains or interferes, asks nothing, and endures all. And to my son, Duane Jr.—you're too young now, but one day you'll understand; and to my daughter, Ashley, one of the most beautiful miracles in my life, one of the greatest joys I can ever know, and one of the reasons why there is a little extra sunshine, laughter, and happiness in my world today—thank you, thank you.

To my mother, Patricia Ann Thompson, and grandmother Alma Echoles, who both rest in eternal peace—each of you forged my personality and share credit on every goal I achieve. I also thank my dad, Eugene, and brother, Derik, who give encouragement in their own particular ways. Thank you. I love you all!

I thank all my friends who shared my happiness when I started Sabrosa Foods Inc. and encouraged me to keep going during even the most difficult times. I would have probably given up without your support and examples of what to do when you really want something.

Speaking of encouragement, I must mention Cheryl Ross, whose patience helped me turn this dream of writing a book into a reality and whose persistence helped me catch and correct mistakes and expound on important ideas. You are a great person and have an awesome talent. I am grateful to have met you. Thanks again, Cheryl!